PREPPING FOR SCHOOL SUCCESS

HOW TO SURVIVE AND THRIVE IN THE EARLY YEARS

JULIE DORE

First published by Ultimate World Publishing 2019
Copyright © 2019 Julie Dore

ISBN
Paperback - 978-1-925884-50-0
Ebook - 978-1-925884-51-7

Julie Dore has asserted her right under the Copyright, Designs and Patents Act 1988 to be identified as the author of this work. The information in this book is based on the author's experiences and opinions. The publisher specifically disclaims responsibility for any adverse consequences, which may result from use of the information contained herein. Permission to use information has been sought by the author. Any breaches will be rectified in further editions of the book.

All rights reserved. No part of this publication may be reproduced, stored in or introduced into a retrieval system, or transmitted in any form, or by any means (electronic, mechanical, photocopying, recording or otherwise) without the prior written permission of the author. Any person who does any unauthorised act in relation to this publication may be liable to criminal prosecution and civil claims for damages. Enquiries should be made through the publisher.

Cover design: Ultimate World Publishing
Layout and typesetting: Ultimate World Publishing
Editor: Richard Burian

Ultimate World Publishing
Diamond Creek,
Victoria Australia 3089
www.writeabook.com.au

Testimonials

'Easy to read, informative and humorous. It could be called the "Parents Handbook on Raising Children". I wish I had it 20 years ago when I was a new parent! As a Primary School Principal for the past 10 years and an Educator for 30 years, I believe Julie gives sound advice. She has touched on every possible topic to provide advice on supporting little people to be the best they can be. I thoroughly recommend this book to any parent, as a "go to" guide, not just in preparing your child for school but for life!'

Lea Martin Dip T, B Ed, Grad Dip Arts, Master Ed Leadership, MBA, Master Dispute Resolution (Principal, Mother)

'A breeze to read and practical advice. Julie has taken the time to map out the maze of the early school years. Her passion and desire for each child's school success is evident throughout!'

**Chanelle Chate
(Speech Language Pathologist)**

'Julie provides practical advice and ideas from both a parent and educator's viewpoint. Delivered in an easy-to-read, non-judgmental way, this book is sure to set you and your child up for success at school. Essential reading for any parent!'

**Matthew Thompson BEd, MBA
(Principal, Father)**

'I just LOVED this book! Julie has hit the nail on the head. Her methods, advice and values are solid, proven and based on common sense, which is hard to find. She has done such a great job of addressing a very, very important yet uncertain future that awaits the next generation. I sincerely loved this book. It was a pleasure to see that there is still hope.'

**Janet Evans
(Swim Teacher, Swim School Owner, Mother, Grandmother)**

'A great book to help ease the transition into school for parents and kids. From what to expect for school interviews, to school lunches and parenting tips. It's all covered. Highly recommend!'

**Dr Renae Dall'Alba FRACGP MBBS BBioMedSc
(General Practitioner, Mother)**

'Wow! Julie has closed the parenting gap we all struggle with… "How do we get our kids ready for school?" It is a tricky path and not one many of us are confident on. But with this book we now have the perfect guide. Julie's knowledge and experience as a teacher and mother have come together in this easy to read book. As a Learning Support Teacher, this is definitely a book I will recommend and refer parents to.'

Elena Bolton BEd (Special Ed)
(Learning Support Teacher, Mother)

'Very informative for parents. I love how Julie relates it back to her own experience. All the ideas to use with kids prior to them coming to school was bang on. The chapter on routines was really valuable - I have even started to use some with my own children. The information on how schools and teachers operate and what parents should consider was excellent. I also like Julie's take on homework, lunches and uniforms.'

Nathan Coverdale BEd
(Deputy Principal, Father)

'A great resource for any parent with a child transitioning into school. Easy to read and covers many important and relevant topics.'

Kelly Littlewood
(Senior Social Worker,
Director of Prepp'd Kids, Mother)

'A practical, helpful guide for families. It will help to make the transition to Prep easier. Julie has captured the skills students need in a great "go-to" book that every family can easily relate to.'

Ann Blakeney BEd
(Early Years Teacher, Mother)

'Preparing your child for school is daunting for any parent. This is a refreshing guide full of important information for those who want the transition to school to be as stress-free and successful as possible.'

Kelly Sheppard BEd
(Acting Principal, Mother)

'As a teacher, one of the hardest things to do is help parents navigate the tricky path that is school. This book offers realistic and practical advice, strategies and helpful tips that support students, parents and teachers.'

Renee Grima BEd
(Early Years Teacher, Mother)

Dedication

For my husband, Shane, who believed in me and
my beautiful girls, Claire and Mia, who made me a mum.

Contents

Testimonials 3
Dedication 7
Contents 9
Introduction 11
Chapter 1 My Story 17
Chapter 2 The School Lowdown 25
Chapter 3 Are You Ready for This? 45
Chapter 4 Behind the Scenes 67
Chapter 5 Street Smart 87
Chapter 6 Fitting In 109
Chapter 7 Don't Worry, Be Happy 125
Chapter 8 Oh Behave 147
Chapter 9 Let's Get Physical 165
Chapter 10 Word Smart 181
Chapter 11 Number Smart 211
Chapter 12 Alarm Bells 223
Afterword 235
About the Author 239
Acknowledgements 243
Special Offers 244
Julie Dore – Speaker 246

Introduction

After teaching for 14 years I thought I knew it all when it came to schools. I thought wrong. Well, not totally wrong, I knew all the 'teacher stuff' but I had no idea about all the 'parent stuff'. People always say there's no handbook when it comes to parenting, even though there are plenty out there. The problem is most of them focus on when your child is a baby. But then what? How do you get them from a baby to school? And successfully? It's just assumed you know what to do once they are about one. It feels like most of the advice says, *'You and your child have survived the first year, you've got this now, good luck!'* And it feels like many of us are still just winging this whole parenting thing, trying to look like we know what we're doing. Then it hit me… we need a different type of parenting book! One with tried and tested methods to make us not only look like we know what we're doing but feel confident that we do. A book to help us better prepare our children and ourselves for school.

So, here it is! A book full of helpful tips, tricks and survival skills for any caregivers to make it through the school years successfully. After reading this book the idea of your child going to school shouldn't be so daunting. One less thing for you as a parent to freak out about. Now when I talk about 'school' in this book I also mean Kindergarten and Prep. Those early years when your little ones are sent out into the world by themselves. And when I talk about you as the parent, it may also be relevant to you as the grandparent, teacher or anyone working with young children. I'll be showing how you can be prepared for school and how you can prepare your child for the best start to their schooling journey. This will in turn help them to succeed in school and allow the teachers to focus on the job of teaching. I've never met a parent who doesn't want to do a good job of raising their child. It's just that raising a child is hard. There are so many things children need to learn; and before you know it they are off to school, and you're left wondering if you've done enough to prepare them.

Often the parent you imagined you'd be and the parent you are, are two very different things. And that's okay. Life is not predictable, and children are certainly not. From a young age their own personalities shine through and each day you'll find yourself adapting or failing to keep up. But there is always hope, we need to be optimistic and believe that tomorrow will be better. And if it's not, well then there's always another tomorrow after that. There are high expectations on parents; some that are very unrealistic. You may feel pressured to keep up with other parents. You can only do so much. Nobody is perfect, and you don't need to be a perfect parent either. Focus on the things that are important, the things that make you

INTRODUCTION

and your child happy, and the things that will prepare them for school. And you will be a good parent. And that's good enough.

Don't compare your child or your parenting to others. Because when teachers look at their students, they don't see their milestones, they see the work and love you put into them. Teachers can't tell who crawled, walked, spoke or who was toilet trained early. They can't tell who was breast fed or bottle fed, or who co-slept or learnt how to self-soothe. They see your child as a person, they know who they are through their words, thoughts and actions. Teachers hear how you speak to your child by how your child speaks to others. They can see which families have good routines, value reading, manners and kindness. These are the things you need to focus on.

You are your child's first teacher. And there is so much they need to learn before they even step foot inside a school. You may not realise it, but teaching is your main job as a parent. And unfortunately, it's often a stressful and constant job with no pay. No matter how hard it may get, quitting is not an option either. Even though you may not have gone to university to become a teacher, here you are, teaching your child every day, teaching them the skills and values that you believe are important. Teaching them how to be a good person, a successful person, each and every day. We were all born to be successful, you just need to help your child to achieve this by providing them with the right environment to thrive in. I will go into these areas more in depth in later chapters, but your child needs a variety of life skills, emotional skills, social skills, fine and gross motor skills, as well as some basic literacy and numeracy skills before they begin school. Sure, you could leave all this up to their teacher, but by then they are already behind and the gaps will only increase between them and their peers.

By five years of age your child's brain capacity is already at 90%! They are more responsive to learning in these first five years of their life than any other time in their lives. Yeah, no pressure, don't stuff up these early years, they are the most important in their learning journey. Surely you want to prepare them as best you can, so they can be confident during their next 14 or so years of school? Parents play an important role in how successful their child is at school. You need to have a positive attitude towards school and instil this in your child from an early age. Your transition to school is just as important as your child's.

If you get even just one useful piece of advice from this book that helps your sanity and your child, I'm happy! I'm a realist. There's no prize for best parent or best child, we're all just doing the best we can with what we've got. And 'good enough' is really 'good enough'. I think there are two types of parents… parents that are struggling and parents who pretend they're not struggling. I hope I'm wrong, but it feels like we all need help, but no one asks for it. We complain about things and

INTRODUCTION

stress about things, but rarely try to change things. We need to share what we know, what we've learnt, to help others. We need to ask for help. This book is me, helping you.

Chapter 1
My Story

PREPPING FOR SCHOOL SUCCESS

Why should you listen to me? Well why not? I'm no parenting expert but I am a parent and I've been there, done that and can save you the painful lessons I had to learn the hard way. I am an expert though when it comes to schools and I do have some great advice to share with you on this mostly unknown world you're about to enter. I read so many baby books when I was having my children as I wanted to be well prepared for this new adventure. Then it came to their schooling and I thought, 'I've got this!' I'd been teaching for about twelve years by then so what did I have to learn about schools? Apparently, a lot! And that is exactly why I'm writing this book for you… being a school parent is a whole other world…

I am a primary school teacher, a mum of two young children and a wife of a husband who works away. I know how to juggle life and even catch most of the balls I'm juggling along the way. I have taught from Prep to Year 7 at a variety of schools and have a Bachelor of Education in Early Childhood Education. Whilst writing this book my daughters are nine months old and five years old. My eldest daughter is in Prep this year and has swimming, gymnastics and Ready Steady Go lessons outside of school. Fun! And my baby girl has swimming lessons and we do Kangatraining together. My husband is a FIFO (Fly-In-Fly-Out) worker who is home every other week. This is the life I juggle.

MY STORY

And then because I wasn't busy enough with two small children I decided to write books as well. I started with a children's picture book called *'Fly in, Fly out'* that helps children understand the jargon that FIFO workers use in a funny way. I love reading picture books as a teacher to my students and love reading them to my children. Writing my own children's book was fun for me to do. Then I had the idea for this book after noticing there was no real information out there to prepare parents and their children for the whole schooling experience. It was a real light bulb moment. I wanted other parents and children to be more confident when they began school and knew I could teach them how to do this. I wish I had known all the information in this book before my daughter started school, I would have been a lot less stressed about the whole thing. And probably could have enjoyed it a lot more too! It's an exciting time but all the unknowns made it very stressful. I had to ask a lot of questions, search the Internet for a lot of things and learn by trial and error. Now everything I learnt along the way I am sharing with you, so you and your child can just enjoy the whole schooling experience.

I want to help parents and children to make their transition to school easier. This will in turn help teachers and schools to focus on the real job of teaching and not waste time on all the other 'stuff' that goes along with new students. It's a win-win situation! You and your child will be better prepared and confident to start the school year and teachers can get on with teaching. You can find some more awesome resources on my website www.preppingforschoolsuccess.com to help you and your child be prepared for school. As well as links to other useful books, workshops and much more!

There's even a section on my website for those who don't have the time or stamina to read this whole book, where I have broken each chapter into dot points. You can thank my husband for this! He started reading my book whilst I was still writing it late one night in bed and told me that it was really interesting and that he wanted to read more but it was just too many pages for him. He suggested instead of a book I could just do a pamphlet for parents to read with lots of pictures. Unfortunately, there's just a bit more to share with you than I could fit in a pamphlet! So, if you're already about to give up reading this book as you're not an avid reader, or you just don't have the time, or you want your other half to read it and know they won't, check out my website for the 'pamphlet version' as my husband would call it.

Life with kids is crazy enough, throw in school and you've got a whole new set of demands. Schools are complex places, and each has their own way of doing things but there are some basics that I will teach you that will help you to survive and thrive! There are things that teachers assume parents know and things they assume kids will already know when they come to school. Kids need to be very independent when they begin school and this all starts with you as the parent teaching them these skills at home. You might think your child is too young to do a lot of things for themselves, but give them a go, they will surprise you. Even if they can only do parts of the things you're asking them to do, it's better than you always doing everything for them. Doing everything for your child fosters dependence and this is the opposite of what your child needs when they start school.

There are so many different types of parents these days and I think I've seen them all and probably been a little of all of them at one stage or another. As your children grow, so do you as a parent. I think children teach parents just about as much as we teach them. And just when you think you've got one age group worked out, they're already onto the next developmental stage, which comes with a whole new set of interesting things to learn. I have learnt that you need to encourage your child to be independent and do things like dressing themselves, toileting and hand washing from an early age. Teachers cringe when they see parents walking in to school carrying all their child's belongings for them like a packhorse or slave. Don't fall into this trap! Kids are very smart at working people out. But they can only go as far as we allow them to go.

Think of your child like a little sponge just waiting to soak up whatever knowledge you can impart on them. They are constantly learning from you, not only through your words but even more so through your actions. Think about how you want your child to be perceived by others and watch what you say and do, as more than likely these words and actions will be repeated by your nearest and dearest. Let me tell you another fact… It is not in the school's curriculum to teach your child basic life skills, such as how to dress and undress themselves, how to use the toilet, wash their hands, blow their nose, use their manners, be kind and say sorry. This is all on you I'm afraid. But don't stress, it's basic stuff that we mostly take for granted as we do it so often that it becomes second nature to us.

I know that it is often much easier and quicker to do things for your little ones, but you are not doing the best by your child. Sure, when they are babies you must do everything for them, but this doesn't last for very long and kids can do a lot of the basic life skills by themselves at an early age. In the beginning however they do them so painfully slow and mostly wrong that you know it would be easier just to do it for them… STOP! Learning to step back and take a breath and watch them have a go at it and learn new things is one of the amazing benefits of being a parent. It's when all that role modelling, talking and helping finally pays off. Don't forget to sit back and smile and enjoy what your mini me is achieving all on their own. Be proud. You have created a little person that can do things. How amazing is that? These are the first steps to creating an independent child, a child that is prepared for school and a child that is going to feel confident in their own abilities.

Unfortunately, I learnt the hard way, that even though I could control a class of 30 students, controlling one child that I created myself was a whole other story. You'd think it would be easy. After all, I knew all there was to know about children. How they learned, how they behaved and why they behaved in certain ways. I had tried and tested behaviour management strategies up my sleeve and was the queen of being calm, confident and consistent with kids. This all went out the window when I was face to face with a tantrum throwing toddler in the middle of the shops! You go blank, everything you know goes out the window, your survival instincts kick in and you go through a whole array of emotions all at once… disbelief, anger, embarrassment. Nothing prepares you for this moment. This is what being a parent is like. You think you know what you're doing one minute and then the next minute it feels like you're drowning.

This is what being a school parent is like too. Just when you think you've got it all sorted out, there's an assignment due tomorrow you didn't know about or they are learning about things in Prep that you still don't know as an adult. It's hard work! And even when they start school you still need to be their teacher, helping them along the way. Too many parents think that it's the school's job to teach their child everything they need to know. But they are only at school, in the classroom, for about five hours a day, and that's on a good day with no interruptions. Now that's about 25 hours a week in a classroom, compared to about 143 hours a week not in a classroom. Now obviously, there's a lot of sleeping going on in these 143 hours, but still, in a week of 168 hours, not a lot of this time is in a classroom. And that's not even including the approximate 12 weeks a year holidays when they are in a classroom for 0 hours a week! The point is, kids are only in school for a small amount of the day and the rest is up to you!

Time flies

When you think about the length of time you actually have your child living with you, it's probably only for about 18 years or so. If you compare this to your whole lifetime of say 80 years or so, it's really not that long. It means you have another 62 years without them living with you. You have, at best, 18 years to prepare them for the world, for life away from you. Take your role as a parent seriously, you are raising a child that you want to be proud of. At the end of the day you want to be able to stand back and say… *'There's my son or daughter. Look at them, what a wonderful human being they are. They are kind, smart, happy and driven.'* And knowing that you helped to create this well-rounded person, will surely be the best feeling in the world. What a wonderful role to have in life, to be a parent, to be able to create a person and then help that person to become a good human being.

Chapter 2
The School Lowdown

Traditions

Make sure you celebrate your child starting school every year by making a bit of a deal about it. Count down days until their first day of school on a calendar, make them a special dinner the night before and a special breakfast on their first day. And don't forget the all-important 'First day of school' photo! Get them to hold a sign that says their grade and the year. You can even buy a pre-made sign that they hold with things on it like, what they want to be when they grow up, what they're looking forward to at school, etc. Make it a bit of a tradition and do the same type of photo every year, they will be nice to look back on and see how your child has grown over the years. Another nice tradition is to buy the Dr Seuss book *'Oh, the places you'll go!'* and at the end of every year get your child's teacher/s to write something about your child in it. Keep this book a secret from your child and present it to them when they finish school as a little memento of their schooling.

Teacher talk

Most schools at present are big on the buzz words 'Differentiation' and 'Innovative Learning Environments (ILEs)'. Firstly, differentiation is using information on a students' learning to make appropriate adjustments. Or in other words, it's when a teacher knows each student and their learning needs and allows all students to experience success and be challenged. Each child is different, and this approach means that your child's needs are being met and this in turn improves their learning. This is a great thing! ILEs are the physical spaces where learning occurs. But it is more than a fancy name for the classroom… it is where schools have built classrooms specifically following innovative space designs and the teacher is using innovative teaching and learning practices. A school can't just chuck a few beanbags in a classroom and remove some desks and say they have an ILE. It is a whole new way of learning and teaching that both the teachers and the students need to be trained in.

The classroom

It's probably been a long time since you were in school and things are very different now. The classrooms are different, the teachers are different, and the kids are different. You can just about throw everything you remember about school out and start again. I had to learn new ways too when I first started teaching and continue to learn new things about teaching each year. Most classrooms don't even have blackboards these days. I say 'these days' and feel about 100, but that's what it's like. It's not just whiteboards that have replaced blackboards, but Smartboards and Interactive Whiteboards. Children use iPads and laptops and sit on beanbags, the floor, sometimes wherever they choose. It's a whole other world! Don't be afraid of the unknown though. The fact that something is different, doesn't mean that it's wrong.

As a parent, you will walk into a classroom with a lot of your own preconceptions about what it should look like, what the teacher should be like, what your child should be learning and how they should be learning it. Do you, your child and your child's teacher a favour and leave these ideas at the door. You will not make any friends by second guessing everything your new school is doing. Sure, you're welcome to your opinion, but unless you are an educator yourself, excuse the frankness, you should probably let the teachers teach. This is your chance to sit back, listen and take it all in. Observe for yourself what is going on, don't listen to gossip, make up your own mind based on how your child is going.

Teachers

Despite what some parents may think, teachers do have your child's best interests at heart. Most teachers I know began teaching because they loved working with children, they wanted to inspire them and watch them grow. They actually love their job and get real satisfaction from teaching. Some days you might find it hard to deal with your child all day, let alone a whole class of them, and these people are actually choosing to do this, and look happy doing so! Teachers mostly run on little sleep, lots of caffeine and shared jokes in the staffroom. And often the reason they have had little sleep is because they were planning for your child's day, marking your child's work or worrying about your child's progress. So please remember all of this before you talk to your child's teacher.

And yes, like every job there are hard days and days they wish they didn't show up to work but for the most part it's an amazing career with positives that far outweigh the negatives. Of course, there is that small percentage of teachers who are just in it for the holidays and the supposed 9am-3pm work hours. Let's just hope your child doesn't get one of those teachers! Luckily, they are few and far between these days and they don't last long in the profession anyway. Teaching being a 9-3 job is a joke and a bad joke at that! A special note: no teacher finds it amusing when parents tell them how easy they must have it with all their holidays, etc. And I mean no teacher! It's a hard gig!

Just remember that they are on your side, they are not the enemy and together you will help your child learn far more than in opposition to one another. Watch how you speak about your child's teacher in front of your child as you want them to respect their teacher and be respected in return. Share important information about your child with their teachers at the beginning of each school year or as it occurs throughout the year. And by 'important' I mean any medical conditions your child has, with their related symptoms and side effects, and any family issues the teacher needs to be aware of like separated parents, family members with a serious illness, or a death in the family. These things can affect how your child behaves at school and their teacher needs to be aware of anything that may be happening in your child's life that could change how they're feeling and behaving. You could also share with your child's teacher any things they are having difficulty with, things that stress them out as well as things they are looking forward to or things they are good at.

Teachers are extremely busy people. They are especially busy just before and after school, so this is not a good time to start up a big ol' conversation about your child with them. Yes, the teacher is quite happy to discuss your child but make a more convenient time to do this, rather than during their busiest times of day when they are settling kids or going to meetings. If you have questions about your child's learning, ask! Don't just complain about it, be proactive and approach the teacher if you have any concerns. They are honestly there to help your child and want you as an active participant in their learning.

When talking to your child's teacher it's important not to let your emotions get in the way of what you're trying to say. Don't mess about with words, get your message across in a polite and direct way, so that you are both on the same page. You don't want to leave a conversation with a teacher wondering if they understood what you were talking about and vice versa. Make an appointment with them if it's an issue that you think is going to need more than a few minutes to sort out. Let them know why you want to meet with them, so they can be prepared for what you want to discuss. This will prevent wasting each other's time. Don't be scared of your child's teacher. They are people just like you. And definitely don't be rude to them! There is no need for it.

Remember they are the ones giving up their extra time, their family time, their sleep, for your child. Be clear on what you want to discuss with them, go in with a list of questions if you need to. Send them this list as early as possible, to give them time to respond. Try not to blindside them with questions you know they can't answer right then and there. Think about why you want to see them and what the ideal result from the meeting would be. And yes, teachers don't tell you everything, there's just way too much to tell. If they had to give every parent in their class a play-by-play of their child's day… well, there just aren't enough hours in the day for that. They won't tell you everything, but hopefully they tell you the important things, the big things. You really don't need to know all the other 'stuff' that goes on.

If it's the teacher that is the problem, see the principal. You don't want to waste a whole year with a bad teacher. This can be very detrimental to your child, not only academically but emotionally as well. Teachers have so much influence in a child's life, for good or bad. You are your child's best advocate. Do what is best for them, not you. On a happier note… there are some wonderful teachers out there, who go above and beyond their job description. And it's okay to let the teacher know if you think they're doing a good job, if your child is enjoying their class, if you like certain things they are doing with the class. Teachers rarely hear positives from parents or anyone, and this would really make their day, if not their year. And give them treats; treats work well too! A happy teacher is a happy class after all.

New year, new rules

A new school year means a new set of rules to follow, especially if you're starting at a new school, but also each time you start a new grade or have a new teacher. The rules change all the time! Just when you think you've got it sorted… BAM!… no packaged food allowed in lunches… or BAM!… this teacher doesn't let you sit wherever you want. Children are more flexible and adaptable than you think, and you need to be as well. Each school, year level, classroom and even individual teacher has their own set of rules. My advice to you is to read the Parent Information Booklet, attend the Parent Information Sessions, read the school's website, ask questions and if you are still unsure ask the question again or ask someone else. You don't want to be 'that parent' who is always sending their kid to school in the wrong uniform, with the wrong kind of lunch, without their homework, etc. You may think nothing of it, but to your child it's a big deal and probably also to the school and their teacher it's a big deal as well.

School lunches

There are a lot of different ways these can be done, but I will share my advice with you. Be organised! Make them the night before to avoid the morning chaos. I've seen people make them on the weekend for the whole five school days! They make five sandwiches and freeze them, cook a treat like cupcakes or a slice and freeze these individually and package up other snacks so they are easy to add into the lunchbox each day. Some parents even have five lunchboxes made up for the week. I'm not this organised but I do like to be prepared. I make sure I have a treat made ready for the week and I pack the lunchbox the afternoon or night before. This way the lunchbox comes home, I clean it out and I repack it for the next day. This is where the acronym KISS (Keep It Simple Stupid) comes in very handy.

Lunches are not meant to be a smorgasbord, a tasting platter or a work of art. They should be simple with things you know your child will eat and can open by themselves. Don't forget those freezer bricks to keep their lunch cool, especially if you live in a warm climate. I have seen so many children try to eat warm yoghurt or meats during a second break lunchtime that it makes me sick. I make them throw them in the bin, which is such a waste, but better than making them sick.

Each school usually has recommendations or rules on the type of lunches and even lunchboxes the children should have. In general, they will need a lunch box and a water

PREPPING FOR SCHOOL SUCCESS

bottle. In addition to these and to make life easier, they will need ice bricks and an insulated lunch bag. Some schools will have fridges for your child's lunch but it's a good habit to get into preparing lunches that can survive on ice-bricks and insulated bags alone for their later school years. If your child has to go up and down stairs to lunch it's best to have their lunch in an insulated lunch bag with a water bottle holder built in and a handle, so they only need one hand to carry it and the other hand is free to hold onto the stair rail.

Some schools are package free schools, so you will need to get a bit creative with your child's lunch. Lunchbox shaming is a thing! Children will be lunchbox shamed by their peers and even teachers. If your school is a package free school, don't stress if all you have at home are packaged foods, just take them out of the package before you put them in their lunchbox. BAM! Package free lunch. Just make sure this is on the very odd occasion.

Some children will be happy to eat the same thing every day for most of their schooling, but others might get sick of this pretty quick. I find it helpful to ask what other children are having for lunch, what they might like to try for their lunch, as well as letting them choose some lunch items when you do the grocery shopping (obviously within reason). If they are telling you their friend 'Sally' has chocolate and sweets in their lunch every day or they want a soft drink that they see at the grocery store, you need to put on your parent pants and say 'no'. But a lunch that has mostly healthy foods with small treats from time to time is perfectly fine. Everything in moderation I say.

Talk to your child about their lunch. What did they like? What did they not like? Did they have enough or too much? You can change it up depending on their answers. Obviously don't fill up their lunchbox with a heap of junk food and packaged foods as this is no good for their growing bodies or brains. There is no point filling your child's lunchbox with a heap of healthy things either if you know they don't like them. If they don't eat it at home, don't assume they will eat it at school. You don't want them throwing their lunch away or eating other children's lunches because they don't want theirs.

If your school has a tuckshop or canteen you could order them something from there as a treat every now and then or on a Friday to give yourself a day off making lunches, just not every day. Otherwise it will end up costing you a small fortune. I like to use tuckshop as a bribe, but that's just me. Some parents are against bribing their children, but I've found that sometimes it works.

Lunchboxes are another hot topic. You can spend a fortune on lunchboxes these days but they all do pretty much the same thing. You can spend as little as $5 to as much as $100. But at the end of the day their function is to hold your child's lunch, not make it for you, no matter how much you spend. My advice to you is to get a lunch box that your child can open easily, that seals well, is easy to clean and holds enough food for them. Get your child to practise opening and closing any lunchbox or container they will be taking to school, as well as opening packets, yoghurt, plastic wrap, etc. And if they can't open it, don't send it! Teachers do not like to open your child's lunch items. Whatever you send their lunch in they should be able to open for themselves. We are going for independence remember. The worst are tins of tuna, what child can open these by themselves? Even I find these hard to open without getting gross tuna juice on myself.

Make sure they know what their lunchbox and water bottle look like and can identify it easily. Add their name, stickers, whatever you need to do to help them remember it is theirs. With water bottles, make sure they can use them easily, have practised filling them up and that they don't leak! Even though schools have water bubblers, make sure your child has a water bottle. Always send them to school with fruit or vegetables of some sort. Most schools have a small break in the mornings, before morning tea or first break, where students are given about 10 minutes to eat some fruit or vegetables as a bit of a brain break. This is because it can be a long time between a child's breakfast and their next lunch break and they cannot learn properly when they are hungry. This may need to be in a separate, easy to access container for a quick classroom snack.

Then there is usually a first break/morning tea followed by a second break/afternoon tea. These breaks give the children some time to eat and some time to play, and again each school is different with the timing and length of these. In general, though, sending your child to school with a sandwich or some sort of savoury food, a few fruits or vegetables, some biscuits and maybe a small treat is quite acceptable. Check out my website for some easy lunch box ideas.

But wait there's more… school lunch warnings! Can you believe I'm still talking about school lunches?! Yeah, they're kind of a big deal. A lot of schools these days are 'nut free' as children have nut allergies, and some that can be quite severe. If your school is a 'nut free' school, this is not a recommendation, but a rule! And yes, Nutella does contain nuts and so does peanut butter, nut muesli bars, and fruit and nut mixes. Yes, you did read that right and might be thinking, *'Well, duh!'*, but these are some of the things that are sent to 'nut free' schools in children's lunches. Schools do not care if your child likes peanut butter sandwiches. They don't want to see another child have an anaphylactic reaction to your child's sandwich. Send them with something else for lunch. If they must have a peanut butter sandwich every day, they can have one after school when it's not going to potentially kill another child.

School uniforms

Enough about lunches already! Let's talk uniforms. As a teacher, I never really thought too much about uniforms, unless a child was not wearing the correct uniform and I had to talk to them about it. Now as a parent, uniforms will be the death of me! There are different uniforms for different days and different socks and shoes and a hat to keep track of as well! I have had to note down what uniform is worn on what day of the week, so I don't get them mixed up and send my daughter to school in her formal uniform on her sports uniform day… this is a big deal to little people! And of course, as a parent you don't want your child feeling like the odd one out as children can be quite mean about anything.

Once you sort out what uniform needs to be worn on what day, then comes the washing routine. You need to spread out your washing days so that your child has a clean uniform each day. At the moment, my daughter wears a school dress on Mondays and Thursdays, a sports uniform on Tuesdays and skorts with a blouse on Wednesdays and Fridays. And this is just one child to worry about! God help all the parents with more than one child at school at a time! Easier if you have boys, then there's no dress or skort option. And even easier again if you just buy five uniforms so you don't have to worry about washing them during the week, but uniforms are expensive!

I had no idea just how expensive uniforms were until I had to buy a few myself and walked out of the uniform shop hundreds of dollars out of pocket. I now know why parents were always paranoid about their child wearing a paint shirt over their uniform for art, changing them out of their uniform in to play clothes when they got home and buying the next size up for them to grow in to. These are all amazing ideas by the way! It's because they didn't want to take out a small home loan to buy another set of uniforms!

Then they also need a spare uniform to keep in their school bag in case of 'accidents'. I recommended buying some second-hand uniforms, especially for the one that is going to sit in their school bag all year and possibly never get worn. Schools often have a uniform shop on site where you can buy second hand uniforms, or you can always try second hand uniform pages on Facebook, Gumtree or charity stores. You can find some in good condition for a very low price. And buy two hats as most schools have a 'no hat, no play' policy and you don't want your child to miss out because their hat gets misplaced or is in the wash.

Write their name on everything! And I mean everything! Their school bag, uniforms, hats, lunch box, containers, water bottles, even their socks and jocks! Everything they bring to school! And make sure your child can recognise their own name in upper- and lower-case letters so they can identify all their belongings. Get your child to help you put their name labels on everything, so they can see what they look like and where their name is located on each. It's amazing what things end up in lost property. And as you now know it all costs a lot of money! Especially if you're constantly replacing lost items.

School bags

A note on school bags… get one that fits ALL of their things inside, so they don't have to carry extra things like their lunch box and library bag as any items not inside the bag tend to get lost. And make your child carry their own school bag for goodness sake! It looks so ridiculous seeing parents walking in to school lugging all their child's belongings and their child walking in without carrying a single item! You're not their Sherpa and making them carry their own bags teaches them independence and organisation by taking care of their own belongings.

School shoes

You may need to buy two pairs of school shoes, a pair of every day shoes and a pair of sports shoes. Try not to buy the cheapest pair as these will not last very long, but you don't need the most expensive pair either. Young children don't think to themselves, *'My parents paid a lot of money for these shoes, I best look after them.'* Go mid-range when school shoe shopping, this way they should last longer and still be comfortable. Children love to scrape the front of their shoes along the ground, get them wet, dirty and best of all, just lose them all together. Then there's rainy days when their shoes will be so wet from the day before that you need to send them to school the next day in their other dry pair.

Make sure their shoes are light, follow the uniform policy of the school (colour and style), and have some room for their feet to grow. If your child can't tie their own shoelaces buy Velcro! Stick with Velcro until they can independently tie their own shoelaces. Teachers don't want to be tying up shoelaces all day and they become a tripping hazard when they come undone. Depending on how quickly they grow in a year, you may be buying more shoes halfway through the school year. Keep an eye out for shoe sales, and stock up. Don't wait until they need the next size. It's inevitable that their feet will grow. Buy some pairs in larger sizes if you know they have liked wearing that brand or style of shoe and it has lasted well. Because no doubt when you need to buy them, they will not be on sale or have the size you need!

School costs

Putting your child through about 14 years of schooling, when you include the Kindy and Prep years, costs a lot of money! State, Catholic and Private Schools all cost money, but can vary greatly on the amount. To give you a bit of an idea of what to budget for one child, for their first year of school, just in school tuition fees, not including stationery and excursions:

- State Schools cost about $100

- Catholic Schools cost about $1,550 + levy fees of about $1,150 for a total of about $2,700

- Private Schools cost about $7,000 + other fees and levies of about $2,500 for a total of about $9,500

- In addition, there's the costly uniforms, school shoes, bag, lunchbox, etc. on top of these prices.

(Note: These prices were from a few schools in the same location, they are very general and would vary greatly depending on your school's location, number of children you have at the school, your income, what grade your child is in, etc.)

This will give you a bit of an idea of what you're in for. It's also good to point out here that if you have trouble with schooling costs you can always talk to the school principal about financial assistance. Most schools offer some sort of financial support to families in need. It can't hurt to ask if you are struggling, and no one else needs to know about it.

Some schools do a bulk stationery order where you pay a fee and all your child's book list items are bought in bulk and delivered to the school. This is an amazing idea and saves parents needing to buy a whole book list of items at the often busy 'before school' sales. You won't even have to bother with laminating, book covering or writing your child's name on all their school supplies. If you've never had the pleasure of laminating and covering numerous books, trying to hide the bubbles in the laminate and getting stuck to things, you have dodged a bullet here! And I especially like the fact that the children can't compare the different types of supplies they have with one another, as they're all the same. No comparing Smiggle items with Reject Shop items, they all have the same! One less thing for children to tease each other about.

Special days

Be prepared for lots of 'special days' throughout the year. There are crazy hair and sock days, dress in certain colour days, free dress days, discos, etc. And most of these need your child to bring in a 'gold coin donation'. Keep those $1 coins in the car as you're going to need a lot of them. Dress in certain colour days are usually easy enough to find clothes for (except when the colour is something out of the ordinary like orange). The dress up like a certain character or theme days are the tricky ones that you'll need to plan for. Don't go crazy and order costumes online though. Your child will probably only ever wear it once, so see what you can put together with things you already have at home or borrow from a friend or relative. There are also class parties that you may have to bring a shared plate to. Keep it simple, children generally don't want to eat anything fancy. Fruit, sandwiches, mini pies, cheerios, etc. are always a hit!

Then there's your child's birthday… cupcakes please! Teachers do not want to cut up a Coles mud cake into 25 slivers for the class to share. Or even better, ice-blocks if their birthday is during warmer weather. And always bring in a few extra for the teachers, teachers love food! If your child has an allergy you could work out with their teacher at the start of the year a compromise on birthday cake days. For example, give the teacher a pack of ice-blocks or some other treat that will last the year, that the teacher can give your child when all the other children are having cake. This way they don't have to miss out on the fun or need medical attention. On the topic of your child's birthday… be mindful when handing out invitations at school, if they are having a party. It's best for you to hand the invites to the parents discreetly. This way you don't offend any parents or children that aren't invited. Unless of course you're one of those parents who invites the whole class to the party! Good luck with that!

Chapter 3

Are You Ready for This?

Picking the right school

When you think about your child at school you probably want two things for them. You want them to do well and you want them to be happy. Whichever you put more importance on, success and happiness are essential to your child's wellbeing. It's important for you as a parent to send your child to a school where they are happy, they feel safe, and they think the other children and teachers at the school are friendly. Picking the right school for your child can be very stressful. You want to make the best choice for them and you usually have to get them into a school at quite an early age. I've known parents who've enrolled their unborn child into a school, so they didn't miss out! Now this is probably a bit extreme but depending on where you live and what school you are thinking of sending your child to, getting their enrolment in early may be one of the boxes you need to tick.

Public schools are generally easy to get into and you usually just have to live in their catchment area. Things get a bit harder once you start looking at Catholic and Private schools. Catholic schools usually enrol siblings first, then look at Catholic families who live close to the school. And sometimes, depending on the size of the school, most places are taken up by siblings with little left over for Catholics and other families in the catchment area. Private schools are expensive and if you have the money to afford them, you are usually safe for enrolment. I would recommend contacting any schools that you prefer and asking them about their enrolment process early so you don't miss out.

If you can be choosey, don't just pick a school that is closest to where you live, pick a school that matches your values and what you want for your child. Pick a school with a safe, inclusive and friendly environment, as well as good academic results. Talk to other parents at the school about the positives and negatives of the school. Approach any schools you are interested in and ask to have a tour of the school. Collect and read the school's parent handbook, you may even be able to get one from their website.

Make sure you go with a list of questions to each school you visit. There's a more complete list on my website but you could ask them about some of the following things:

- Parent involvement
- Academic results
- Extracurricular activities
- The learning environment
- Class size
- Teacher turnover
- Fees
- Homework
- Transition program

A school with a high teacher turnover each year is usually a bad sign. The school may also have some questions for you and your child, as they too are seeing whether the school is going to be a good fit for you. They might assess your child's readiness for school. This can help them to see whether the school can cater for your child's needs and get to know more about your child. You can also check out schools at www.goodschools.com.au to compare schools in your local area.

School interview

It's important to prepare your child for their school interview, but not to put too much pressure on them. You can get them to practise talking to other adults and answering simple questions for themselves. Practise some general things with your child, like their name, age, birthday or other questions about themselves. Play games with them to help them identify letters, numbers, shapes and colours. Get them to practise writing their name, drawing pictures, counting to 10, saying the alphabet, singing songs and listening to stories. Ask them questions to get them thinking about things like, what they like to play, eat, do, read and things they don't like.

Ask your child whether they're looking forward to going to school and what they think school will be like. Practise getting them to following simple instructions and answer open-ended questions. In the interview they may just observe how your child behaves. Remind your child that it's okay to be nervous but everyone is there to help them. And of course, dress nicely, be on time and put your phone on silent for the interview. Answer questions honestly and be polite. First impressions are important.

My husband was a bit blindsided when we went to our first school interview and he was asked if he had any questions about the school. He looked at me with his 'deer in the headlights' face, as if to say you did not tell me I would need to talk, and replied, *'This is Julie's thing. I don't really have any questions.'* It might be a good idea for both parents to be aware that they may both be asked some questions in the interview.

Below are some questions they may ask you. Plus, some good answers to go with a few…

- What are you looking for in a school? (Be honest, but appropriate)

- Why do you want your child to come to this school? (You could answer with, *'Your school has a good reputation in the community'* or *'Your school comes highly recommended'*)

- What values do you like about this school? (Check out their values on their school website)

- How can you help at school? What skills do you have that may help the school? (Involved parents and parents who volunteer are desirable)

- How would you describe your child? (Focus on the positives, but don't lie or carry on too much)

- What do you know about this school? (Refer to your research from the school's website)

- Have you applied to other schools? (Do not rank the schools you're hoping to get into, simply say you're looking at a few)

- What's your occupation?

- Is your child toilet trained? (Yes, is the answer they're looking for, if the answer is no, you have some work to do)

- Has your child had all their vaccinations? (Again, yes is the answer they're looking for)

- Does your child have any needs that we need to be aware of? Or do they have any needs that may affect their learning or how they access the curriculum? (There's no point pretending your child is fine if you know they have issues that may affect their learning. Schools cannot reject your child on this basis, that is called discrimination. Just be honest. You want a school that can cater for your child's needs)

And of course,

- Do you have any questions about the school? (Try to think of a couple or simply, *'No, I did have but you've managed to answer them all'*)

Parenting styles

Your parenting style will have an influence on your child's behaviour and development. How you interact with, support and discipline your child, will determine whether they grow up to be healthy, happy and successful adults. No pressure… You might feel as though you have no 'parenting style' or it changes from time to time. There are three main parenting styles, see if you can identify with one, more than the others.

Firstly, there are authoritarian parents. These parents are strict, have boundaries and rules, which the child is expected to follow, and react to situations with shouting and punishments. If you prefer an image for this style of parenting, think drill sergeant. It's I say what goes, my way or the highway and children being raised through fear of their parents.

Secondly, there are permissive parents. These parents are the polar-opposite to authoritarian parents. They are easy-going, don't demand things but instead offer choices, have few boundaries or rules, and are warm and loving. Think hippies, parents as friends, and children who do what they like.

And lastly, there are authoritative parents. This is the ideal parenting style. These parents are in-between authoritarian and permissive parenting styles. They set boundaries and rules but also let their children have choices and learn from their mistakes. They encourage them to be self-reliant and they help their children to regulate their emotions. This authoritative parenting style tends to raise children who are more independent and happier than the other styles. It's where we aspire to be.

We can't simply fall back on, *'Well that's how I was raised'*, *'It didn't do me any harm' and 'I turned out fine.'* Your child is not you, you are not your parent and times have changed since you were raised. You and your partner need to make a conscience decision on how you want to raise your child. It can be hard as you probably come from different belief systems and were raised in different ways. And you may even have issues of your own that you need to deal with before you deal with your child. How we understand our world comes from our experiences, which become our beliefs, then our behaviours. Share with your child the parent you'd like to be and explain to them your role as the parent, your values and rules. And listen to what they want you to be like as a parent. This is a wonderful conversation to have with your child. It can help them better understand why you say and do the things you do.

Parent helpers

You need to be an 'active participant' in your child's learning, but that doesn't mean being in the teacher's face all the time. On the one hand, you can be too involved, and your child will be sick of the sight of you. And on the other hand, you can be not involved enough, and your child will wonder why all the other parents are there and not theirs. Work out how you can be involved in the school in some way. Whether you can volunteer your time, skills or money. It's all appreciated. You want your child to be independent. This is hard to achieve if you're always around, so give them room to find their own feet. Choose a few events each term that you can attend to show them that you're interested in what they're doing. Don't volunteer for everything or nothing, balance is the key!

Your child's age is important in this too, young children love seeing their parents at school, older kids not so much. Don't become a 'helicopter parent' hovering over your child with everything they do. Know when it's time to 'cut the cord'. Let your child's teacher know you're keen to help if you can and see what kind of vibe you get. Some teachers are very guarded at the start of the year as they don't know you or your intentions for coming in to help. Unfortunately, some parents only want to come in to 'help' to compare their child to the other children, get information to use as gossip or to make their child look better in the teacher's eyes. This kind of 'help' is not needed.

There are so many ways that you could be helpful in your child's classroom if their teacher is open to it. Such as, helping with messy activities that require more hands, listening to children read, making resources, or helping with supervision for special events. And if you can't help during school hours, due to work or other commitments, you can always join a school committee that has meetings at night. Or on the other hand if you are a super busy parent that has no time to help at your child's school, see who else you could rope in. This could be their other parent, another relative or friend with some spare time on their hands.

All they need is one familiar face turning up to show them they are special. You could even do a deal with another parent that you know in your child's class and tag team events with them. This means having another child with you at special school events as if they're your own, paying them the same attention as your child, taking their photo, etc. This way when there's events that you can't attend for some reason, there's another school parent that you can rely on to be that fill in parent.

Eyes and ears tested

Before your child starts school get their eyes and ears tested to rule out or help any issues they may have. Speaking, listening and reading are major areas of learning and you don't want your child falling behind because they couldn't hear the sounds correctly or see the words properly. Children adapt very easily to their surroundings and they could easily be getting by, by copying the other children in the class, if they were not hearing or seeing clearly for themselves. We got our daughter's hearing tested before she started school and I don't know if it was good to hear that she could hear really well, because now I know she's just ignoring me when I tell her to do things. No, I'm kidding! Of course, it's good that she has great hearing, and now we're working on her 'selective hearing'.

Hair

Hair is the fun part of school mornings. Not! If you have boys, you are very lucky! What fun it is! Said no sane mum ever! The brushing, the knots, the whining, more knots, more whining, the knot spray, the hair ties, clips, bows, headbands, ahh! It's a nightmare! It's best to have their hair tied back and this is usually a school rule if it's past their shoulder. A ponytail is good but a braid or a plait is better to help avoid getting nits. You can even give it a spray with a nit prevention spray to be extra careful. Nits are no fun at all! I hope you never receive a school note that says 'a child in your child's class has nits, please check and treat your child's hair'. This is the worst note to receive as a parent; well one of the worst. You then need to check your child's hair, just about one strand at a time, looking for microscopic nits and eggs. Then treat it, which children hate, and wash all the sheets, towels, etc. as well. And pray that no one else in your family has them.

Every child is different

One of the worst things you can do as a parent, is to compare your child to other children. What's the point? What are you going to get out of it? They'll either be worse, which will make you feel bad, or they'll be better. What are you going to do with that information? Don't worry about where your child is compared to other children. It is your job to make sure they are achieving the best that they can be. Don't worry about what reading level they're on, or how neat their writing is compared to others. If you feel they could be doing better than they are, practise with them at home. Like I said before, there's only so many hours in a day that they're at school and the rest is up to you, you're their first teacher. And never talk about your child's lack of abilities in front of them, this is very disheartening for them to hear. You are probably the one person that means more than anything to them and to hear you making fun of them or putting them down must feel terrible to them. What is this going to achieve, other than making them feel bad and crushing their self-confidence? There's no need. You are a grown up, their role model, their safe place. Be kind.

Bending the truth

Children say the darnedest things. And some flat out lie! Don't take everything your child says as gospel, find out from both sides what actually happened. Talk to their teachers if you have any concerns, with the mindset of sorting things out, not blaming others. Sometimes your child, other children and even other parents like to bend the truth in their favour. Don't assume teachers are aware of an issue your child has told you about, as your child might not have told the teacher about it. For instance, you will look a bit silly if you say to the teacher, *'This child hit my child'*, then when the teacher finds out what actually happened, it could be that it was your child who was in the wrong. It might seem harsh but when a child tells me that another child has done something to them, I always ask them, *'And what did you do?'* Even with my own child. As in, *'What did you do before they hit you?'* and *'What did you do after they hit you?'* This way you don't jump to conclusions about what happened and who is in the wrong. It's best to get all the facts first.

Teach your child that if they have an issue at school they are to tell their teacher first. The teacher is there to help them, they are the one at school, they are the one that can sort out problems between children at school. And if they don't do anything about it, tell a different teacher. Don't wait until you get home to tell someone about it. With schools comes gossip, some parents live for the stuff! Often schools have a group of parents they like to call, 'The Carpark Mafia'. These are a group of parents that hang around in the mornings or afternoons to gossip about school. It's like they have no job to go to and no life to be had outside of school. They love talking about other parents, other children, teachers and most of all how great their own child is. Stay clear of these parents! If you see them heading your way, run! No good will come of interacting with them. They are only out for more gossip. Note: There are also nice parents who sometimes hang around before or after school, you will quickly work out the difference.

Making parent friends

Your child will not be the only one having to make new friends at school, you will be making parent friends too. Be open to having a casual chat with the other parents in your child's class. If you are a shy person, this may seem very daunting. But you need to put yourself out there. Again, be the role model. You should be encouraging your child to talk to the other children and make new friends, so take your own advice. Word of warning though… you want to make the 'right' parent friends. Not like the ones in 'The Carpark Mafia' I described earlier, usually ones that your child is friends with their child, or you would like them to be, is a good start.

Make friends with parents that will have your back, not talk behind it. Get their phone number as one day you may need to ask them for a favour. This may be that you're running late, stuck in traffic or whatever and you need them to watch your child for a few minutes after school. Maybe there's school events on that you can't remember the details of or you've misplaced school notices that you need to ask someone about. Whatever it may be, schools are crazy places and it's good to have someone there you can rely on. And don't forget to return the favour. Friendships are a two-way street, you can't just take without giving. Your parent friends will become your support network. And we all need that!

Parent talk

Children are masters at mimicking their parents. They really are, 'Monkey see, monkey do,' as well as, 'Monkey hear, monkey say', so be careful what you do and say in front of them. Although it does make for an interesting day in the classroom, your child's teacher doesn't really want to know what interesting words you yelled whilst driving. Remember, whenever you are with your child it's like someone is monitoring your every move. It's not only yourself and your family that you need to worry about them copying inappropriate things from, it's also your friends, their friends and even what they see on screens. I think L. R. Knost says it best, *'Sticks and stones may break bones, but words can shatter souls. Choose carefully the words you say to others. Choose wisely the words you say to yourself. Words have a way of becoming truths we believe about ourselves. And what we believe, we become.'*

So be very mindful of how you speak to your child, especially when you're in a bad mood. Always pretend there is someone else in the room and would you speak to your child like that in front of them, and if the answer is no, then don't. Words can hurt their feelings and they are often not as resilient as us and they often don't understand why you're being mean to them, when you're the person who is supposed to love them unconditionally. Unconditionally is hard, they will test your patience, a lot, but remember you are the adult, you are their role model… act like it. Keep it positive in front of them. Don't put them down, belittle and ridicule them. You are better than that! Plus, you can always vent to your friends and partner about them later, out of their ear shot, just for your sanity. And remember the wise words of Peggy O'Mara, *'The way we talk to our children becomes their inner voice.'*

Child safety

I want to talk about a very important topic that a lot of us used to refer to as 'stranger danger'. Some of us may still use this term but it's a bit misleading. It implies that only strangers are the ones that we need to be worried about, and this is rarely the case. A lot of the time children are hurt by people they already know, not strangers at all. We need to teach children about 'tricky people'. As in, if an adult is asking you for help or to go with them somewhere, they are being a 'tricky person' and should not be trusted. We teach them that no adult needs help from a child and you shouldn't believe them or go anywhere with them. The Daniel Morcombe Foundation has a lot of useful information on child safety, check it out at www.danielmorcombe.com.au. There's a whole section with 'Keeping Kids Safe' resources that you can use with your child. They will be learning about it in school, but it is a very important subject that you should also be teaching them at home.

Something else that your child needs to be aware of is the correct name of their private parts. Children come to school with numerous, often very interesting names for these and it can be very confusing for them when a teacher tells them what the parts are called. If you have a son, teach them that their private parts are called their penis and testicles. And if you have a daughter, they are called their breasts and vagina. Their mouth and bottom are private parts too. Teach them that their private parts are only for them and 'trusted people' to see and/or touch. Your child's list of 'trusted people' will be people like their parents, other family members, their teachers, doctor, etc. These people will vary slightly from child to child, so discuss them with your child, and when and why they would need to go to these people.

They need to have at least five people that they can trust and know they can talk to about anything. Don't forget to listen to your child when they are telling you something. No matter how trivial it may seem to you, it is important to them, and this is why they're telling you. Don't ignore what they're telling you, because if this happens too often, they will stop telling you things. They won't see you as someone they can talk to, and then when there is something they really should tell you, they won't. Don't wait for it to be important stuff in your eyes, as it's always been important stuff in their eyes.

The parent trap

Parenting is hard! You want your child to like you, but you also want them to respect you. Sometimes you can't have it both ways and at the end of the day always remember that you're their parent, not their friend. I know that sounds a bit harsh, but it's true. Think about what a friend is… someone who enjoys doing the same things as you, likes to do fun things with you and has the same interests as you. You may have these things with your child, but you still need to be the one who says no, teaches them right from wrong, gives them rules to follow and consequences if they don't. And this is a lot different to a friend.

You can sometimes feel like you have a split personality as a parent, you must be the good cop and the bad cop all in the one day, sometimes in the one sentence! You need to be the person they not only love but trust, respect and listen to. If you're worried that you're doing a bad job as a parent, you're probably like the other 95% of parents that feel this way. But bad parents don't stop and worry about how they're parenting, they just do what they like with no thought about how it is affecting their child. So, if you're reading this book, I'm certain you're not a bad parent. You're trying to help your child succeed at school after all, go you! This should surely be a parent's main goal… to help their child succeed in life, to be the best that they can be and to provide them with unconditional love and support to achieve their dreams.

Don't try to be the super parent. You can't do it all and you shouldn't try to either. Sorry to burst your bubble. You don't need to join every committee or sign your child up for every club there is. There are not enough hours in the day to do everything. Between school, before and after school activities, work, chores, meals, rest and sleep, where do you fit it all in? Instead of trying to do everything and half-ass everything, why not do less things and do them well. It's a real juggling act being a parent. Don't worry about keeping up with the Jones's, worry about keeping yourself and your family sane and happy.

Give yourself a break

Don't forget to do things for yourself. It's easy to lose sight of who you are when you become a parent. It's almost like you have to put your life on hold while you make sure your child has a great life. No. Your children are an extension of you and should add to your life, not take from it. Make sure you have time to yourself, some 'me' time to do things that you enjoy. You need it to recharge your batteries and be happy. You cannot look after your child well if you are not 100% there yourself.

Yes, as a parent you are going to get run down, tired, annoyed, stressed, worried, and about a million other things… so give yourself a break! Take time to breathe. Do it now…breathe in…and out. See? Slow down, it's good for you. Sometimes it's hard when you have a million things running through your head and a child that won't stop talking but try to be in the moment. Remember to stop, look around, enjoy where you are. And don't worry, there will be a lot of other emotions like feeling happy, proud, excited, silly, and amazed for you to experience as a parent as well.

Quality time

Above all, your child simply wants your time, that's how you show them love and that's what makes them happy. You will need to spend time with them if you want to develop a good relationship with your child. They need to know that we have time for them. Having our attention is something children thrive on. If we take the time to just be with them, it allows us to see the world through their eyes. It makes them feel valued and that you understand them. Even though sometimes life gets in the way and we have lots to do as a parent, they need to know that we always have time for them. When spending some quality time together, it's important to tell them when time will be up and when the next time together will be.

It's also important that each parent makes time to spend with each child. And if you have more than one child, you want to find some time during the week where you can spend some quality time with each child by themselves. This way they don't have to fight for your attention or fight with each other. They have you all to themselves. Even if it's for just 20 minutes a week. This can make the world of difference to your relationship with your child. Spoiling children with material gifts is no substitute for spending quality time with them, doing things you both enjoy and listening to them.

Chapter 4
Behind the Scenes

Having good routines and 'training' your family members to follow these routines is important. Mornings can be hectic and so can evenings. Routines make sure everyone is on the same page, doing what they need to be doing and getting everything done quickly. You could use a chart with your routines on it where your child can visually see what they need to do. They could tick each job as it's done or simply use it to check if they've forgotten anything. This will also save you repeating yourself a million times, every day, like Groundhog Day. You can simply say, *'Check the chart.'* Younger children could have a picture to represent each job to be done or words for older children. It can be as simple or complex as your family needs. You could have columns for each child if you have more than one child, or separate charts for each child. A magnetic whiteboard is easy to set up with a routine on it and your child can use a whiteboard marker to tick off jobs or use magnets to cover jobs as they're done. Check out my website for examples of routine charts.

Have a practice day and pretend it's the first day of school… get up, have breakfast, get dressed, brush teeth, do hair, pack school bag and, if you're really keen, drive by their school. Aim to do it all within a reasonable time and with everyone still smiling at the end of it. You may notice some creases that you need to iron out before the real day. And if you're timing the run to school, make sure you consider what traffic will be like on a real school morning.

Morning routine

Not every parent or child is a morning person, but we need to remember that how we start our day largely determines how the rest of our day will be. If we can have a successful, productive morning this will set us up for a successful, productive day! Make sure your child knows the morning routine and what they are expected to do. Depending on your child's age and abilities, when they wake up on a school morning their routine may be… make bed, have school clothes on bed ready to put on, help make breakfast, eat breakfast, brush teeth, get dressed, do hair, put sunscreen on, pack school bag, put bag in the car, and get in the car.

Breakfast

Make sure everyone has a good breakfast! It really is the most important meal of the day. If you are running late and don't have time to sit down and eat breakfast, take it with you to eat on the way to school or even at school. Do not skip it! Breakfast gives your child fuel for their growing bodies and helps them to stay focused on learning at school. Your child cannot concentrate and learn properly if they are hungry. And if your child is like mine and wakes up at 6am, it's a good 3-4 hours before they get a snack at school. That's a long time to wait if they haven't had any breakfast. It doesn't have to be a big, fancy breakfast either, just fruit, yoghurt, toast or cereal are all easy, healthy options.

Be on time

Having a good morning routine should mean you get to school on time. Running late is very stressful for everyone. Parents are often yelling and very short with their children when they are running late and this in turn puts your child in a bad mood. Plan to leave about 10 minutes before you actually need to, just in case life throws you a curve ball. This curve ball could come in the shape of breakfast being spilt everywhere, surprise homework found in a school bag or missing car keys. Then there's also the chance of delays on your way to school, like traffic jams. Being at school on time gives your child time to settle in, do any morning jobs they need to and relax a bit in the school environment before the bell rings. This is a much calmer start to the school day and sets them up to be in a good mood and right mindset for the rest of the day.

It is also important to be at school on time for academic reasons. Just missing 10 minutes of school per day, adds up to 50 minutes per week, about 1.5 weeks per year and about half a year over their 13 years of schooling. I might be pointing out the obvious here, but good school attendance goes hand in hand with success at school. Learning is progressive and when your child misses a day it may be hard for them to understand the work the following day, as it leads on from the day they missed. As the parent, you need to model the importance of regular school attendance and discourage missing school.

Drop offs

School drop offs… think of it like 'Pulling off a Band-Aid', do it quickly so it's over with. Don't hang around with your child until after the school bell, this does not help them separate easily and it certainly does not make you any friends with the teachers. Leave. Just leave. Don't drag out goodbyes and hugs and kisses and whatever else you think is helping them, just go. It's hard enough to settle upset children of a morning without their parents still being there. Children like to put on a big performance for their parents and pull at their heart strings. Believe me, it doesn't take them long to settle down after you go, but the delaying of you leaving is what can set them off. This doesn't mean that you sneak off while they're not looking either, this can be worse. Set up a short goodbye routine with your child that you do each time you leave each other. Just a simple goodbye, one hug, one kiss and an, *'I'll see you this afternoon'*, is all you need. Short and sweet is best. I have more on helping your child deal with separation in Chapter 12.

Homework

Now for the h word… homework! The word that makes parents, children and teachers all cringe. Most parents hate doing homework with their child, most children hate doing their homework and most teachers hate planning and marking homework. But we all just have to suck it up and do it! Homework allows parents to see what their child is doing in school and how well they are understanding the work. If your child is struggling with their homework, maybe you need to talk to their teacher about it. They have obviously not grasped the concept and need further practise with it. Homework should be a follow on to what the children are learning in class and skills they need to practise.

Reading should always be a part of homework as it is a skill that needs to be practised every night. Doing homework allows children to independently practise new skills they have acquired, as well as refine skills they already have. It sets them up to be lifelong learners with self-discipline, good study habits and time management skills. Some schools have a 'no homework policy' and some teachers do not give homework. This may seem like an ideal solution to the homework problem, but this does not help your child succeed.

As a parent, you should take homework seriously enough not to let your child hand in some half done, messy rubbish that is below their capabilities. But you also need to make sure you are not doing it for them. Believe me, teachers know when you are doing your child's homework for them. And what's the point of you doing it? It's a waste of the teacher's time making and marking it, and your time doing it. It teaches your child they don't need to take pride in their work, that cheating is okay and doing school work is optional. Don't see homework as another chore, make time for it in your daily routine, it is important.

Yes, it may not be fun for everyone but that's life! Your child needs to learn to do the things they don't enjoy quickly and correctly, then they will have more time to do the things they'd rather be doing. Homework may seem trivial when your child is young, but it will become more difficult later on and if they already have basic study skills, this transition will be a lot easier. At a young age, afterschool activities should include a lot of downtime, play, family time and time with friends, with some homework in there as well.

Get your child to do their homework straight after school, maybe after a snack or while they have a snack. They may be tired after a long day of school but it's better to get it over and done with rather than dragging it out between any TV watching, other activities, dinner, showers, etc. Other activities can be used as incentive to get the homework done faster. Make sure your child has a quiet area to do their homework without interruptions and that they understand their homework.

Before beginning their homework, get your child to tell you what they need to do, so you can check their understanding. This will save having to re-do it all later. Get them to do all the parts of their homework that they can do before asking you for help. Then make sure you're only helping them, not doing it for them. Perhaps do some examples with them on a separate piece on paper until they understand it. Check their homework before it goes back to school. There's no point in sending back homework half completed or all wrong.

Night-time routine

Depending on your child's age, a night-time routine for them could be… help prepare for dinner, eat dinner, help clean up from dinner, dessert, shower, brush teeth, toilet, read books, and lights out. The bedtime routine needs to be calm and consistent to wind them down, with no screen time for about an hour before bed. They should have no food or drink right before bed and their bedroom should be quiet, calm and dark. These are good sleep habits and ones you should be modelling yourself. Every child needs to read, every night. If your child says they have no homework, and you check that this is true, get them to read for 10 minutes or so, depending on their age.

Get into the bedtime routine of reading each night with your child. Read aloud to them, no matter how old they are. When you read aloud you model the correct pronunciation of words, punctuation and expression to your child. It shows them that reading is a lifelong skill and of course it is valuable time spent with them. Reading non-picture books to your child forces them to use their imagination to create the story in their minds as you are reading it to them. Don't forget to discuss the book with them, before, during and after reading it. I'll talk more about reading in Chapter 10.

Sleep

A big part of any night-time routine is getting your child to bed at a decent hour to give them enough sleep for their age.

A well-rested child is a better behaved and happier child, they smile more and argue less. Sleep is so important for children. It is when they grow, repair their bodies and develop their brains. A bedtime of 7pm, with at least 11 hours' sleep, is best for young and school aged children. Each child will vary in the amount of sleep they need to be well rested. Some young children will still need naps of an afternoon, after a big day to recover from a busy week. Even a 20-minute nap in the car on the way home may be all they need to recharge their little bodies again. Make sure they don't have a nap too late in the day though, as this will interfere with their bedtime and it could be a fight to get them to sleep.

Bedtime can be a hard time with a lot of complaining and stalling. My daughter went through a fun stage of epic stalling tactics, after all the bedtime routine and lights out, she would come out numerous times with excuses for the toilet, a drink, another hug, another kiss, forgot to tell us something, sore leg, itchy back, another I love you, etc. It drove us nuts! But we've since learnt that if she has a busy day and no afternoon sleep, she goes to sleep straight away. We've also had to set bedtime boundaries. She does her night-time routine and then before she is finally tucked in we say to her, *'Go and do all your jobs'*. This means she does anything that she's forgotten to do, like have a small sip of water, go to the toilet, say goodnight to other family members, tell us one last thing, etc. She is then tucked in and knows not to come out or call out as this will mean she misses out on something the next night, like dessert or an extra story.

Children need enough sleep to be switched on during the day and to ultimately succeed at school. Sleep is vital for learning, remembering and functioning properly. Children who aren't getting enough sleep are not only tired, but cranky and cannot do their best, just like their parents! Sleep underlies all areas of development and it's not just important to have a good amount of sleep (quantity), it also needs to be a quality sleep. Watch your child sleeping and see if they're an 'open mouth breather', if they snore or you can hear their breathing, as these can all be signs of sleep problems.

There are a lot of children who have sleep problems or a lack of sleep and this affects them negatively in so many areas. Bad sleep habits can cause behaviour and health problems. Behaviour problems such as poor concentration, lack of focus, being anxious, and a lack of enthusiasm. Health problems such as being overweight, having delayed growth, poor immunity, poor coordination, and a lack of energy. Bad sleep habits can also negatively affect your child's memory and communication skills. So yeah, sleep is kind of a big deal! Treat sleep as sacred, for all family members.

Meal prep

The school week is busy and planning meals ahead of time helps everyone. Every household is different, but I like to sit down on a Saturday morning and plan my family dinners for the following week, Sunday to Saturday nights. Then do the grocery shopping on the weekend and buy all the food for the week. I often ask family members what they would like for dinners and have a flick through some cookbooks or websites for inspiration. I also have a list of dinners on my phone that my family enjoys, they are easy to make, and I know they will eat. And I've included a dinner list on my website to help you out as well.

Planning for meals has also saved us a lot of money! We used to get takeaway and eat out quite a bit before I started planning weekly meals because it used to get to an afternoon and no one would know what they felt like for dinner or feel like cooking. And I don't know about you, but I hate when you ask your family what they want for dinner and they say, *'I don't know'*… ahh, it drives me nuts, well it used to before I started meal planning. My other bit of advice would be to, *'Cook once, eat twice.'* This way each time you cook you are cooking enough food for two nights and whether you have it the next night or freeze it, that's up to you. I only cook every second night, so this means I cook on a Sunday, Tuesday, Thursday and Saturday. Only Saturday as there is an odd number of days in the week! But this means only cooking dinner on two school nights! I like to put any afterschool activities we have on the meal planner and if I know we're going to be home too late to cook one afternoon, I plan to have leftovers that night. I love leftovers! It means a night off cooking, woohoo! It's like a free-pass.

Chores

Chores, love them, hate them, we all have to do them. Yes, everyone in the family should have chores to do. Even young children can do basic chores. And I think the trick is to start them young and get them into the habit of doing it. This shows children that they have a role to play in the family and they are a valued member of the family. Plus, you don't want to be doing all the chores yourself! Often the jobs we do as parents are monotonous, boring and thankless ones. Share the fun around I say! Take some time to list down all the chores that need to be done in your household and then share them out. You might even divide the list into own and family chores. As in, there are a lot of things that we each need to be doing for ourselves, like putting our clothes in the laundry, cleaning up our mess but there are also family chores that need to get done and these can be divided up between family members.

Use a chore chart to keep track of all the chores that need to be done and who does them. Obviously, the amount and type of chores everyone does will depend on their age, abilities and time. Even if you're lucky enough to have your

BEHIND THE SCENES

own cleaner or you are a stay at home parent, there are still jobs that your children should be doing. Chores like picking up after themselves and putting things away can be done even by two-year-olds. It teaches them life skills, how to do things independently and to take pride in their belongings. Plus, most classrooms have jobs that the children need to do each week, just like chores. And you don't want your child whining about having to do a class job, as they've never had to do jobs at home before. These could change weekly in their class and they will need to do things like take messages to the office, hand out/collect items in class, and take/collect the tuckshop. They will also have to keep their area tidy, put their belongings away and rubbish in the bin daily. And they should come to school knowing how to do these things already.

Cleaning together can be fun. I know you're rolling your eyes by this statement but stay with me. Make it fun or a bit of a game when they are young and don't expect perfection from them. If you've asked them to make their bed and they have, no matter how messy it looks to you, leave it. You're going to have to lower your standards. But if you are a bit OCD like me and can't stand it looking like that, go and fix it up, but only when they don't see you doing this. This is important as why would they bother making their bed again if they know you're just going to do fix it up or do it again for them? We're not aiming for perfection by getting them to help, we're hoping to develop good habits. A good rule is, *'You make a mess, you clean it up.'* My daughter chants it now like a mantra, when I say, *'You make a mess…'*, she replies, *'You make a mess, you clean it up.'*

Teachers also use little songs and music to help children clean up. They may have a clean up song they sing like, *'Everybody clean-up, clean-up, clean-up, everybody clean-up, just like (insert child's name here).'* Or simply play an upbeat song and call it, 'The Clean Up Song', so when they play that song in the classroom, the children know it's clean up time. Some children hate to clean up, with a passion, but need to learn that this is a part of playing. Yes, it's fun to pull every toy out and play with them, but you need to clean them up at the end. It's also a good habit to get them into packing up each game after they've played with it and before moving onto the next game. This way there isn't a massive mess at the end to clean up that is overwhelming for a small child.

Sometimes you will have to help them a little, and by 'help' I mean help, not doing it all for them. You don't want to get into that habit. Children are smart, they will see you cleaning up all their mess and think, *'Oh, why do I need to clean up if they can do it all for me?'* You can even make it into a little game or a challenge, *'Let's pick up five things each'* or *'You pick up the blocks and I'll pick up the puzzles.'* Or buy a timer to use so they can see they have two minutes to clean up. You'll be amazed how much they can get done in two minutes! Timers work great for many things you want them to do quickly. You could even pretend that the toys are talking, *'Hello, where are all my block friends, I miss them, can you please put them all back in the box with me?'* Use funny voices, animal voices, whatever you can think of to make it fun. These can also work to get them to do any boring things or things they don't want to do. Whatever works is my motto!

Children will appreciate all the jobs you do a lot more when they are doing some of them as well and respect the need to keep the house tidy if they are having to tidy up too. Every household will have a different list of chores but there are a lot of things we will all have in common. Chores include making beds, taking clothes to the laundry, washing/hanging out/folding/putting away clothes, setting the table, cleaning up after meals, preparing meals, making lunches, taking the rubbish out, putting bins out, packing the dishwasher/washing up, dusting, cleaning windows/bathrooms/toilets, sweeping, vacuuming, mopping, mowing, whipper-snipping and vacuuming/washing the car. And this is just to name a few!

Then if you have pets, there's a whole other list of chores that will need to be done. Phew! You can see why we need to share them around. 'You are not a slave!' Say this mantra to yourself daily if you need to. Children, and all family members for that matter, are quite capable at doing many things that you are probably currently doing for them. Test them out, see what they can do, I'm sure they'll surprise you. Or, on the other hand, they won't, and they'll be lazy. And if this happens, you'll just need to put on your parent pants and tell them what to do. I'd rather be the parent that 'reminds' them to do their chores than does the chores for them.

Extracurricular activities

If your child has after school activities, these may also need to be prepared for in the morning. Put these on a weekly plan so your child knows what they're doing each day. There are a lot of extracurricular activities these days that your child can be involved in. But how do you choose the right one for them? It's hard when they are young to know what they would like to do, as they can't exactly tell you. And then even when they are old enough to tell you what they like, do they really know if they've never done it before? Maybe they've just seen Angelina Ballerina and now they want to do ballet, or their friend does gymnastics, so they want to do it too.

Thankfully a lot of sports and other extracurricular activities allow children to have a trial class. Almost like a try before you buy scenario. Which is great, as some of these activities can end up costing you a small fortune. Especially if you have to buy uniforms and equipment as well as pay fees. You don't want to be forking out heaps of money for an activity that they soon lose interest in after a couple of classes. If you want to get your child into an activity at a young age, a lot of the time it will be finding out by trial and error whether that activity is right for them. It might just be best to wait until they are a bit older and really know what they're interested in. Or to see what they enjoy doing with their friends and join an extracurricular activity with a friend who shares the same interests as them. You may find you are overwhelmed by the number of choices you have, or you may be limited in your choices due to your locality, the times they are on or costs.

Your child might simply do an activity as you or other family members do it and it's convenient. Just make sure that this is in the best interests of your child and it's something they want to be doing and are not just being forced to do it. You need to think, who is this really for? You or them? Try to use their natural talents and strengths to work out how you can enrich them with extracurricular activities. Be careful you don't try to get your child in to too many activities as this can be very stressful for you and them. Over-scheduling can put a lot of pressure on families, on their time, finances and their emotions. While some children will thrive by doing many activities, others will feel anxiety and stress.

You need to work out a balance and what works for your family. Think quality not quantity. This allows your child to still have down time, play time and time with family and friends. You need to remember that when they are little they get tired easily and need their down time. You need to be aware of how your child's activities whether they be after school or on weekends, will work around other things like meals, homework and other family members. It's also okay for them to be bored. They don't need to have a busy schedule at such a young age. Allow them to be bored as it creates imagination. On the other hand, there is nothing wrong with having high expectations when it comes to your child, just make sure these expectations are realistic for your child and your bank account.

Downtime

Don't forget to plan some downtime and fun into your routine. Just like school, work, chores, meals and after school activities are part of your routine, downtime and fun should be too. Downtime is everyone having some time to slow down, relax and take a breath. What this looks like is different for everyone. Downtime could be things like reading a book, sitting outside, going for a walk, listening to music, watching TV or having a nap. It could be by yourself or with others. We need fun in our lives. Doing things that make us happy, that make us smile or laugh. That take us away from the boring parts of our routine for a bit and remind us that life is good.

Fun is something different for everyone and some things you think are fun, will be anything but for others. Some ideas of fun things to include in your routine could be... going out for a meal, catching up with friends or family, playing a sport, exercising, going to the beach, seeing a movie, going to a show or visiting somewhere new. These activities make great family times, the times your child will remember. It shows them that you're human, you're a person just like them that likes to have fun and take a break. That you're not just the person who looks after them, tells them what to do, takes them places, cooks, cleans and works.

Try to plan some fun activities to do on weekends and holidays. It doesn't have to be anything expensive and you don't even need to leave your home to do them. Just the fact that they got to do 'something' is enough. Often after a weekend or holiday they will be asked by their teacher to either talk or write about what they did. And it's hard to talk or write about something if you haven't done anything. Some teachers use this as a writing activity every Monday morning. How disheartening for your child to write each week 'On my weekend I did... nothing.' And then they get to sit there and listen to all the fun things their peers did. Fun! So, give them something to write about! Like I said before, it doesn't need to be anything expensive, you don't need to go on a plane somewhere or spend hundreds of dollars on something. It's simple things like, a sleepover, a movie night, dinner outside, going to a park or a playground, riding bikes or scooters, or just playing games that will give them things to talk or write about at school. As well as make some of the best childhood memories.

Chapter 5
Street Smart

Being independent

I talked about this a little already... but teach your child to be independent. By the time your child starts school they should be able to do many things independently, and if they can't, you need to take a step back and give them a chance to do things for themselves. You'd be amazed at how many things they can do for themselves, if you just let them. Within reason, obviously. You don't want them doing things that are not safe for their age or abilities. You can foster their independence by getting them to do activities on their own, such as drawing, making things, organising their things, pretend play, puzzles, listening to music, looking at books, or playing with playdough.

Get them to practise new things they will need to do at school like using water bubblers to drink out of; these can be tricky to use if they haven't done it before. Get your child to practise opening and closing their lunch box, other containers and their school bag. Children are not a blank slate when they come to school, they bring with them a lot of life skills already. Every child learns and masters skills at different times and as needed, but there are some general life skills that your child should have before they start school. And most skills need to be practised many times over before they perfect them.

Children tend to live in the moment, whereas adults are always thinking about what comes next. This is probably why we may feel as though we are always rushing our child to get onto the next thing, but they don't see it as important as us. The concept of time is difficult for young children to understand so it doesn't really matter to them. They would rather just finish what they're doing than jump up whenever you say it is time to. Children move at a different pace to adults, and sometimes that pace seems glacial. And it's always when you're in a rush, and the more of a rush you are in, the slower they go. It's almost as though they can sense it, *'Oh mum's in a hurry, I should pretend I'm a sloth and do everything as slow as I can, this should help'*... not!

I think we tend to talk a lot as parents and we're always telling our child what to do. I think instead we need to get them saying what they need to do and owning it. Instead of telling them what to do, ask them, *'What do you need to do on a school morning?'*, *'Where do you put your plate when you've finished dinner?'*, or *'Why don't we stand on the couch?'* Getting them to say what they need to be doing saves you saying the same thing over and over. It can also stop you being ignored, they can't ignore themselves and hopefully it will sink in more when they say it and then it becomes a habit. Stranger things have happened...

Swimming

Before I get into all the life skills your child will need for school I want to talk about teaching your child the very important life skill of being able to swim. So many children are not being taught this fundamental life skill from an early age. The Royal Life Saving National Report 2017 says, *'Children under five are most at risk of drowning. An average of 30 children under the age of five have drowned in Australia each year for the past 10 years.'* This number is crazy! From 2019 all Queensland state primary students are required to have a water safety or learn to swim program. However, participation in these programs is not compulsory, meaning parents can choose for their child not to participate.

Why is this even a choice? It should be compulsory for all children to have swim and water safety lessons from a young age. No child is drown-proof. Make sure you always supervise your child and teach them about water safety. Even better, have a qualified instructor teach them swim skills and make sure you know resuscitation. Go to www.kidsalive.com.au for more information on water safety. Their website has heaps of free resources for parents and children. The earlier you teach your child to swim the safer and less afraid of the water they'll be. Not only that, swimming is fun and great for your child's health and fitness.

Brush your teeth

Firstly, your child needs to brush their teeth and gums every morning after breakfast and every night before bed. You should supervise their teeth brushing until about the age of eight, to ensure they're using the correct technique for a good amount of time. I know… that's a lot of years! Some things to consider… only use a pea size amount of toothpaste, brush in a gentle circular motion and replace their toothbrush once it begins to fray. And dentists recommend introducing toothpaste to their brushing only after 18 months of age. As soon as your child gets teeth you can use a damp cloth to clean them. You can explain to your child that brushing removes plaque and prevents tooth decay and gum disease. Some children hate brushing their teeth or just don't want to. If this is the case, you can make it into a little game with them, do it together or even better… show them gross pictures of people who haven't brushed their teeth on the Internet as an incentive. Works a treat!

Go to the toilet

Next is toileting, this is a crappy job (pardon the pun), but someone must show them how to do this properly. Children should be able to use the toilet independently, including wiping their own bottom before they get to school. Because no matter how nice your child's teacher is, they are not going to wipe your child's bum for them! I'm sorry, it's just not a part of the job description. They need to be taught each little part of using the toilet, and there's a lot of steps when you break it all down. It includes… taking off clothing, sitting/standing in the right spot, getting all your wee/poo in the toilet, wiping the correct way, making sure you've wiped it all away, putting toilet paper in the toilet, flushing it all away, putting clothes back on, and washing your hands properly. Let your child practise going into a public toilet stall by themselves, and using the toilet, including using a urinal for boys, wiping, flushing, and putting clothing back on, all by themselves. This is good to practise as it is what they will need to do independently at school.

Your child needs to be able to identify when they need to go to the toilet, ask to use the toilet when needed and use it correctly. Teach them not to wait until they're busting to ask, as it may be too late to make it to the toilet then. Or even better, to go after a lunch break before they go back into class, just in case. Just like you get them to go before a long drive in the car, they may be in class for the next two hours, so it's best to have a try. Better safe than soggy... I mean sorry. Make sure you use polite language when talking about toileting, like bathroom/toilet, poo/poop, wee/pee, instead of all the other rude words that we know for these things. Because children being children, will repeat them at school and get in to trouble for saying them.

Get dressed

Your child needs to be able to dress and undress themselves in their school uniform. This will include zipping and unzipping zips; doing up and undoing buttons; pulling up and taking off underwear, shorts, skorts, skirts and socks; and putting on and taking off dresses, shirts, singlets and jackets. As well as being able to put on and take off their school shoes, whether they are slip-on, Velcro, buckle or laces. Do not, I repeat, do not send your child to school in shoes they cannot put on and take off independently. It takes children some time to master tying their shoelaces, it's a tricky skill, let them master it before you rush out and buy them school shoes with laces, that they cannot do themselves. This is not a teacher's job. There is nothing worse than having to do up a child's laces and realise they are wet, it hasn't been raining and they have just come back from the toilets! Gross! This is one of the low points of being a teacher… getting children's urine and faeces on you. Yuck!

So please, please practise all the above dressing and undressing skills with your child, numerous times throughout their young lives. Get them to put on their whole school uniform, including socks and shoes and walk around in it all for a bit to get used to it. Getting all dressed for school can be a painfully slow process for a young child but try to resist the temptation to step in and do things for them to hurry them up. Allow some extra time for them to do it themselves, you are teaching them to be independent. It's best not to watch, it's like that saying… *A watched pot never boils*… well *A watched child gets dressed in slow motion.* This can be super frustrating on a busy morning, walk away, do your morning jobs and just check in every now and then with encouragement as needed.

Dress for your climate

Get your child into the habit of putting on sunscreen and a hat when they go outside. I'm always mindful of being sun smart as where I live in North Queensland, Australia, it has one of the highest rates of skin cancer in the world! Every two out of three Australians are diagnosed with skin cancer by the age of 70. How scary is that statistic! Make sure you model being sun smart. This includes wearing appropriate clothing, hats, sunscreen, sunglasses and choosing shady spots to play. There are some things you can do to help your child become more sun smart. When they are getting dressed you can remind them that they'll be playing in the sun today, so what would be a good choice of clothes to wear? Have hats where your child can see them as a reminder to put one on, like near the door or near their car seat.

Teach them how to apply sunscreen themselves by putting a bit on each cheek, their nose, forehead and chin, then rubbing it in. Being careful not to get it near their eyes and that they wash their hands when they're done. Teach them to also put it on any other bits of skin not covered by their clothing. Get them to be 'shade detectives' to help you find shady areas where they can play. Check out www.SunSmart.com.au for more tips on being safe in the sun. The website also has animations, videos, songs and online books and games to teach your child about being sun smart in a fun way. Alternatively, you may need to practise putting on extra layers with your child to keep them warm, if you live in a cooler climate. Coats, jackets, boots, gloves and beanies can all take time to master getting on and off and practise makes perfect!

Use your manners

Children know how to eat from a young age, but you need to teach them how to do this using good manners. You will have plenty of time to practise table manners with them over the years as you share meals together. Make sure your child can use a spoon and a fork correctly and drink out of a cup and water bottle properly, before they start school. Other things like chewing with your mouth closed, not talking with food in your mouth and not putting too much in your mouth at a time, are all important as well. Get into the habit of washing hands before eating and washing hands and around mouths after eating. You want these hygiene practices to be second nature to your child, and this takes repetition, reminders and often nagging on your part, for them to become a habit. It's amazing how messy a child's face can get from the simplest of foods, this is where washing around the mouth comes in. You don't want them spending the rest of the day with their face covered in food.

Make sure they know to wash their hands after they've been playing outside too. And make sure they're not just wetting their hands under the tap, but rubbing them together, with soap preferably, for a good amount of time, until they are clean. Teach your child to cough and sneeze into their upper arm or sleeve if they don't have a tissue. So many children are taught to cover their mouth or nose with their hand and so many germs are spread from hands. You don't want them sneezing or coughing into their hand and then wiping it elsewhere or touching food with these same hands. Gross! Be proactive, schools are full of germs.

A little bit of good manners at school goes a long way. Teach your child the basics, like saying 'please' and 'thank you', from a young age and then repeat about a million times until it sinks in. Other ones that are good to model and practise at home include 'pardon me', 'excuse me', 'may I' and 'good morning/afternoon'. As well as waiting for their turn, being patient and lining up nicely. It's just about being polite and it teaches them good social behaviour that will help them their whole life. Good manners are also about sharing, asking to use things and not grabbing them, cleaning up after yourself, listening, using a quiet voice and respecting property. And saying sorry and apologising when you are in the wrong. It's the Golden Rule… *'Treat other people as you wish to be treated.'* And these are all things you need to be modelling and practising with your child from a very young age. Remember, children are like tiny versions of you; they hear and see everything you do. If you want them to be polite and well-mannered, guess who else needs to be?

Respecting yourself and others

Another basic life skill is teaching your child how to look after their belongings. Teach them to respect not only their own but others' property. This means not leaving things lying around but packing them up after they have used them. And when they are using something, teach them to take care of it and use it carefully in the correct way. Children can often get rough when playing with things and forgetful at times. But they can be taught how to look after things. Practise playing with things nicely and for their correct use, and putting things away where they belong, not shoving them into the closest hidey hole.

Discuss the need to look after our environment, and why this is important. That we need to put our rubbish in the bin and not just throw it on the ground, as this is called littering and causes pollution. There are some very disturbing photos of turtles caught in plastic and other rubbish that has made its way into the ocean, just search the Internet for some pollution images, if you need to really get the message across to your child that keeps littering. Remind them that it's their world that they will need to live in for a long time to come, and it's up to them to keep it clean. It all comes down to respect, for themselves and others.

Another aspect of respecting others is teaching your child about 'personal space'. They need to understand that everyone has their own personal space and that when we're talking to other people we don't get right in their face or on top of them. We give everyone, including other children, adults, teachers, a bit of room so we don't get in their personal space. And we leave a bit of room between ourselves and others, so we don't have other people in our personal space. This is important when sitting or standing near others.

Speak up

Your child needs good communication skills before they get to school to make sure their needs are being met. They need to know who and how to ask when they need help or have a question. Remind your child that it's always best to try to do things for themselves first but sometimes they will need to ask others for help. They need to make sure they use a confident voice and tell people exactly what it is they want. Get them to practise with you and other adults. If the teacher is busy, they need to see if there's someone else that can help or wait patiently for the teacher. If it is something urgent, like they are badly injured or busting to go to the toilet, it's okay to call out for help so that people know it's an emergency. You may need to clearly define what kind of things are an emergency. I will talk more about how you can help your child with speaking in Chapter 10.

Listen

Listening is another very important skill to practise with your child. They will miss a lot of learning, information and directions if they cannot listen and do what others are telling them. Plus, it is just very rude if your child is not doing what they've been asked to do or just ignoring others. You should be expecting them to listen and do what you tell them at home and teaching them that this is exactly how they should behave for their teachers at school. If you show respect for others, they will show it in return, hopefully! They need to be 'active' listeners, not just sitting there staring into space. They need to be quiet to listen but being quiet doesn't necessarily mean they're listening. You need to do regular checks for understanding to make sure they are 'taking in' what is being said. A good habit to get into is to get your child to repeat things back to you. Even if they don't say it word-for-word, by doing this, they show you they have understood what has been said.

From the age of one, your child should be able to follow basic instructions, such as, '*Stop.*' Then when they are about three they should be able to follow two-step instructions like, '*Go to your room and get your hat.*' As they get older and their vocabulary and understanding increases, you will be able to give them more detailed instructions. Make sure your instructions are always clear, specific, age-appropriate and simple. Wait until you are near your child before you give instructions and you can see they are listening. There's no point yelling to them from another room when you can't even see if they're listening to you. Give your child some time to process what has been said to them. Don't repeat yourself straight away, wait and watch for understanding and compliance. More on listening in Chapter 10.

Hands up

Teach your child that when they're at school they will usually need to put up their hand to speak. Explain to them that there are lots of other children and everyone wants to be heard but if everyone talks at the same time, no one can be heard. If they put their hand up, people know they want to say something. Warning... teaching your child to be resilient is so important, as sometimes they won't get asked, even when they've had their hand up for a 'long' time. This may be for many reasons, such as someone else says what they were going to say, or time runs out. No matter how good they thought it was to share, they may not get to share it. This is life! They need to learn to not take it personally, and that these things happen.

And again, if it's an emergency and they've been sitting there with their hand up waiting to be heard, they may need to call out. I've had a child wet themselves while sitting with their hand up waiting for their turn to talk. When you need to go, you need to go and sometimes acts of nature come before manners. It's a bit hard to practise 'Putting up your hand to speak' at home, as you may feel like a bit of a dork, but play pretend 'school', where you can only speak if you've put your hand up and someone says your name. It also teaches your child patience as they wait for their turn to speak. Some children put their hand up ALL the time, for anything and everything, be sure to teach your child that you don't need to tell everyone everything that you think. That it's okay to let other children have a turn to speak. I think the Dalai Lama said it best when he said, *'When you talk, you are only repeating what you already know. But if you listen, you may learn something new.'*

Sit still

Sitting still. You'd be amazed at how long some little children can sit still for. And then there's others who, as soon as their bottom hits the floor, they wiggle like a worm. Each child has a different attention span and it will depend whether they're interested in what is in front of them, as to how long they can sit still for. In general, children up to five years old have a limited attention span, with four- and five-year olds being interested in an activity for around 10-15 minutes. Children need to be able to sit at a desk with feet flat on the floor, as well as sit with their legs crossed on the floor at school. These are skills that need to be practised with your child. They don't come naturally and it's best to model them correctly. Good luck!

Try your best

Children will work out very quickly that they are good at some things and not others. And that other children will be better or worse than them. You need to instil in them from a young age to just 'Try your best'. No one can ask you to do more than your best. Their best may be different to what you expect, and that's okay. They also need to be in the habit of 'having a go' before they ask for help. This helps them master new skills and perfect old ones, as well as to not be lazy! It's so easy, and almost an involuntary action for a parent, to jump in when you see your child needing help. Don't! Give them a chance to work it out for themselves. They may surprise you and get it done by themselves, or maybe just get further than they did before, or just flat out fail.

Remind them that things are always hard before they are easy. And that anything worth learning takes time. I feel like I'm just shooting off sayings here, but they are all so relevant! It's better than calling them *'Unco'* (short for uncoordinated) or whatever you may be thinking at the time, as they miss kick the stationary ball for the eighth time. The important thing to encourage is, 'Don't give up' or be like Nike and 'Just do it'. Explain to them that yes, it may be hard now, but by giving up, it will always be hard. On the other hand, by practising and trying again and again, they will get better at the skill and it will get easier. Hopefully…

I'm bored

It's important to remind your child that sometimes they will find things 'boring', but sometimes in life, you just have to do things that are boring or things you don't want to do. News flash… not everything we do in life is fun! It's best to teach them that if they find something boring, do it quickly to get it over with, rather than dragging the time out longer and whining about how 'boring' it is. Or if this can't be done, remind them it won't last forever, and fun is just around the corner, hopefully! And, if they do it well the first time they won't need to spend even more time doing it again. When children get to school they will be expected to participate in class activities, even when they don't want to or are not interested in the activity. They will still be expected to sit, listen and engage like the rest of the class.

You can work on these skills with your child by going to free events that libraries, shopping centres and other community groups put on, where they will need to sit, listen and do things like, watch a show, listen to a book or music. Or even sign them up to do some pre-school lessons like swimming, gymnastics, dancing or a sport. These activities will allow them to interact with children of a similar age to them as well as have times when they will need to sit still and listen to their coach. You can also just get your child to do activities they don't like from time to time, as when they get to school they don't get to choose every activity they do.

Tech savvy

Children these days love technology. Or at least all the ones I've met! (There I go, sounding like I'm 100 again!) They are usually good at navigating their way around devices, like tablets and mobile phones, and are often better at it than their parents. But don't forget to teach them how to use other forms of technology, like a computer as well. Even if you don't have a computer at home, you could buy a keyboard that works with a tablet or just go to your local library and use a computer. If you can practise the basics of using a computer with them before they start school, this will save them a lot of time in class. I've often had computer classes with younger children where half the time, if not more, was spent getting them to type their name to login, and they had it in front of them to copy.

They need to be familiar with what the alphabet looks like in all capital letters, like on a keyboard. As well as what some of the other keys are. Just having a practise in a blank document gives them a chance to see what it all means. Using a mouse takes some getting used to as well, especially if they're just used to using their finger on a screen. One of my favourite sayings is, *'Technology is amazing… when it works.'* Yep, it's not always reliable and they need to be patient with it. Not sit there pressing the same key repeatedly and expecting it to go faster, as children do. When in fact, this only makes it go slower as now it must do that same command many times over once it catches up.

General knowledge

Life gives us many 'teachable moments'. Every day there will be opportunities to help your child learn something new. Or even to expand on things they already know or even just to check their current level of understanding. This may come under the term 'general knowledge'. Just information that young children need to know, often learnt through repetition and time. Things like knowing their first and last name, their age, street address, birthday (month and day) and telephone number. The last one may be a bit tricky when they are little, so you can always just focus on the emergency number '000' to get them by. They need to be able to recognise their own name and learn how to write their first and last name in the correct case, as in a capital letter (upper case) for the first letter of their first and last name, and the rest of the letters in lower case.

Teach them how to 'say' the letters of the alphabet, rather than 'sing' them. And that all these letters are called 'The Alphabet'. Sometimes the song makes 'lmn' sound like one letter, and then some children sing 'w, x, y, n, z' with either 'n or and' in there. Talk to your child A LOT to improve their vocabulary and general knowledge. Just by talking to your child about and describing things you both see, they can learn the names of body parts, colours, shapes, letters and numbers. It's as easy as pointing out things and naming them, get your child to repeat the name and in no time at all they will know what it is called.

Practise drawing with them, not just with a pencil on paper, use your imagination, draw on an app on a device, with chalk on the footpath, in the sand, wherever and with whatever you have available. Model and get them to copy drawing basic shapes, a person, letters and numbers. They can even begin by tracing over yours before they do their own. Drawing helps with their visual motor skills, how the eye collects and understands the information it sees, and then uses this information to manipulate objects with our hands. Visual motor skills are essential to everything we do in life.

Draw a few of the same shape or letter with one 'odd one out' and get your child to find the 'odd one out'. This will help with their visual discrimination skills, by recognising similarities and differences between objects. Some other activities to help your child develop their visual discrimination skills include: sorting objects according to one attribute (e.g. colour, size, shape), sorting objects from around the house (coins, cards, socks, etc.), playing matching and memory games, dominoes and 'find the difference' puzzles.

Practice makes perfect

All the skills in this chapter, and in this book really, just need to be practised with your child until they come easily and automatically. Don't give up when things get difficult, anything worth doing is worth doing right! This applies to you and your child. We can't make good habits stick overnight. Teach your child to use common sense to find solutions to problems they encounter. Don't always jump in, give them time to process and try it their way first. A saying I like to use is, *'Common sense… is not that common.'* They will need to learn common sense through trial and error, unfortunately. But this allows them to learn something new from every situation.

They need to be able to accept correction and learn from it. Otherwise they will be doomed to keep repeating the same mistakes. Remember a mistake is not a mistake if we learn from it. And growing up is just a learning journey, isn't it? Our children don't enter this world with all the information they will ever need to know already programmed into them. There is a lot they will need to learn from the time they are born to the time they enter school. Think about how far they come from a tiny, totally dependent baby to the little person you send off to school. It's crazy how much they have had to learn.

Chapter 6
Fitting In

Just like any skill worth learning, learning social skills takes time. Luckily your child has a few years before they start school to work on their social development. They are going to need all the help they can get when they enter school and are faced with the realities of school life. Don't get me wrong, school can be a very happy, fun and interesting place for children. But unfortunately, it can also be a place where they will encounter bullying, teasing, loneliness and social isolation. These can all be very hard to deal with when your child is feeling a lot of emotions all at once, in a new environment, and you are not there to comfort them.

The best thing you can do for your child is to prepare them with the skills to handle any negative situation that comes their way. Whether your child is confident, shy or in between, they need strategies to deal with social issues that are bound to arise at school. They need to be allowed to make their own decisions from a young age, however trivial they may be, so they can learn to make positive choices in a safe environment. If they can learn by trial and error, how best to solve their own problems at home, these will be valuable skills for them to use at school.

Problem solving

Bad things are going to happen to your child, let's be realistic, you can't wrap them up in cotton wool and be with them 24/7 to make sure they are always protected. You can't fix all your child's problems for them, you need to teach them how to fix their own problems. It might sound a bit harsh, but school can sometimes be sink or swim and survival of the fittest. It's your job to prepare them to handle bad situations on their own. And know the difference between something they can handle on their own and something they need adult help with. Either way, you want them to come to you with all the situations they have, you want to hear about the good, the bad and the ugly.

Show them you are interested, even when you're not, brainstorm with your child solutions to problems they may have, so they can see that not all is lost and there is always something we can do to make a situation better. But don't be too quick to jump in and give all your solutions and try to persuade them to the solution you like best. You need to encourage your child to pick the solution that they will try, they need to own their decisions and feel empowered by doing something about it. They are the ones, at the end of the day, that will need to put the plan into action, so they need to feel comfortable in doing so and feel confident that they can. And then, if it all works out, they can feel proud that they could sort out their problem. And, if it doesn't work out, as can happen, they know there are other options available for them to try tomorrow.

Your child may come to you with a problem that happened at school or maybe they keep doing something at home that you want them to stop. When you are sorting out a problem with your child you must first acknowledge their feelings. You then describe the problem briefly. You can talk about your own or other people's feelings in the problem to get them looking at it from another person's point of view. Then ask them for ideas that they have to fix the problem. Listen to all their ideas without rejecting any, no matter how silly you think they may be, and add in any of your own. You can then decide which ideas you both like and get rid of any you both don't like. You will be left with a few solutions. Try them out.

Hopefully the first works, but if not try another one. If you've tried a few and they haven't sorted out the problem, go back and come up with more ideas to try. Once your child is at school and they are having a problem that you can't solve between the two of you, make sure you talk to their teacher about it. This may give you a better insight into the situation at school, as all you had to work with before was your child's version. It is good for your child to try and sort their problems out for themselves but if they have tried to resolve it and couldn't, definitely seek help from the school.

Social stories

A good way of preparing your child for social situations at school is to role play social scenarios or stories with them at home. Get your child to suggest solutions to a problem. The problem can either come from you or ideally, they can come from your child. They may be things they've witnessed or things they've made up. Situations like, *'You are hit at school, what should you do?'*, *'You don't understand your work, what do you do?'*, or *'You are hurt, angry or sad, what do you do?'* Or check out my website for more examples of social stories to try with your child, as well as good books that deal with social issues. Make your role play realistic by giving your child a favourable ending as well as an unfavourable ending, as both could occur, and they need to be able to handle rejection. No matter how nice your child tried to handle a situation, you can't control how other children will react and behave.

Watch your child in social situations, don't be creepy about it, just notice how they speak to others, their actions and reactions. Use these for later discussions, like *'I loved how you got off the swing and let the other little boy have a turn, that was great sharing.'* Or *'When the girl said you weren't allowed to play; how did that make you feel?'* Discuss any good choices they made and praise them for these and discuss times they could have made a better choice and what they could do or say next time. These little chats can tackle issues like manners, sharing, turn taking, following rules and many more social issues. And what's even better about them is they are relevant to your child and fresh in their memory. There's no point bringing up an incident that happened weeks ago or even days ago and talking about it with them, as they probably won't see the connection. Children have very 'busy' lives and it's hard for them to remember what they did a few hours ago, let alone a few days ago.

Listen to your child

When your child tells you things, don't ignore them. I know, it's hard, they say a lot of 'stuff' and a lot of it is random stuff but listen to them anyway. Don't just ignore them with statements like, *'Oh, I'm sure it's not that bad'* or judge them with statements like, *'Why didn't you…?'* You want them to feel safe and supported when they talk to you. You want them to come to you when things are bothering them. No matter how insignificant it may seem to you. But if all they get is ignored or judged, they will soon stop seeing you as someone who supports and listens to them. You are your child's advocate. You, more than anyone else, should be able to know when they need your help. It's important to also notice how your child acts when they are happy, on what I'd call their 'good' days. This way you will be able to tell when they are having a 'bad' day from their actions, or lack of. And then you can help them sort out whatever it is they need help with.

One of the biggest things our children want from us is our attention. Surely, we can spare some time in our day to give them our undivided attention. That's the tricky part… 'undivided' attention. Parents are busy people, we are busy before school and we are busy after school, but these may be just the times when your child wants to tell you the important 'stuff' they need to. Give them your full attention, not while you're looking at your phone or cooking dinner. Make time for them. When a child must fight for your attention they will often use negative behaviour to get it. Obviously if they are fighting for your attention, just asking you hasn't worked, so they bring in the big guns, as any attention is good attention.

Good or bad, it's all attention to them. This may come in the form of yelling, tantrums, or whatever fun thing they know really gets you going. Just like you know them, they know you. They know how to press your buttons and get the best reactions from you. And when they need attention, sometimes they need it right then and there. You'll stop a lot of bad behaviour from just giving them some attention when they need it, when it's reasonable to. Trust me on this one! *'Every day in a hundred ways our children ask, 'Do you see me? Do you hear me? Do I matter?' Their behaviour often reflects our response.'* L. R. Knost.

Another way you can listen to your child and show them you are interested in what they have to say is to ask them about their day. If you ask them, *'What did you do at school today?'*, they will inevitably answer, *'Nothing'* or *'I can't remember.'* Instead ask them more social questions like, *'Who did you play with today?'* or *'Who was nice to you today?'* By asking them these types of questions you can find out how they're going socially and who are in their friendship groups. Talk about their feelings, what feelings they had during the school day. Again, reassure them that having these feelings is okay, especially if they're negative feelings, but remind them it's what we do with these feelings that counts. Ask them what they did when they got angry, sad or embarrassed. Talk about appropriate ways to act on our emotions.

Your child needs to feel heard, that you listened to what happened to them and were non-judgmental about it. Make sure you always ask them open-ended questions to encourage them to have a proper conversation with you. Don't just ask, *'Did you have a good day at school?'* with them answering, *'Yes'*, and conversation over. You should know a bit about what subjects they have each day and you can ask more specific questions, such as *'What did you write about today?'*, *'Tell me three things you did during sport today?'*, *'What was the best thing that happened today?'* or *'Who did you sit with today?'* Show a genuine interest in their day and share your day with them to model good social language.

Play

Young children learn a lot of useful skills through play. Never underestimate the power of play. 'The United Nations Convention on the Rights of the Child' lists play as one of the basic rights of every child, that's how important it is! Play helps young children understand their world, their relationships with others and their place in the world. Through play they learn by trial and error, they develop communication skills, confidence, problem solving and concentration skills. When playing with others they learn how to interact, share, take turns, work together, negotiate and use conflict resolution skills. Play is essential for your child's well-being and for their emotional, social, physical and intellectual development.

Sometimes play can get loud, messy and annoying, but so can life, and through play your child is learning to deal with life. If you can't stand loud and messy, get your child to play outside where it's okay to be loud and messes are easier to clean up. Children need time for unstructured play. Don't pack your child's day so full of activities that they have no time to just play. They don't need a lot of expensive toys to play with either. The best toys are not necessarily the most expensive, they are the ones that allow a child to use their imagination and keep them engaged.

Your child will go through stages of play as they get older. Mildred Parten Newhall named some stages of early play. The first stage being 'Unoccupied play'. This is when your child is simply exploring objects and shows a very short interest in an object at a time. Like when you see a baby pick up a toy, hold it for a little bit and then put it down, grab the next toy and repeat. Then they move to 'Solitary play', where they play alone, and this can be up to the age of two. They seem to be unaware that there are other children present and are not interested in what other children are doing. Then there is 'Onlooker play' where they are watching other children play, they may be physically near them, but they don't join in with them. It's almost like they are learning what to do by watching others, they are simply taking it all in. Next is 'Parallel play' where, at around two to three years of age, they may be playing close to other children but still not with them. They may sit with other children who are playing with blocks, they will also play with blocks, but their play will have nothing to do with the other children.

Then there is 'Associative play' where they play with others, they learn to share and cooperate. They might sit with other children and do puzzles together and find pieces for each other, or colour in together and share the colours. And finally, for young children, there is 'Cooperative play'. This is usually after three years of age and when they are interested in other children. They play roleplay games together and play games that have rules, but these 'rules' may not always be followed. These stages are progressive, but your child can always move between each stage when situations change. For instance, they may be in the 'Cooperative play' stage but in a new environment they might prefer to engage in 'Onlooker play' until they feel comfortable with their new surroundings.

Pretend play enhances creativity and outdoor play improves their risk-taking abilities, can help overcome anxieties, and

FITTING IN

is good for their physical health. It's also good to play games with your child that have one person coming out as the 'winner'. Be careful not to always 'rig' the game so your child is always the winner. This teaches them nothing and does not prepare them for school. It gives them an unrealistic view of their abilities and an inflated ego. You want them to obviously experience winning, but they also need to experience losing, as this is what will happen when they play games at school, and you want to see how they react in both situations. Are they a gracious winner or do they gloat? Are they humble in defeat or a sore loser? Watch their words and actions, and later comment on how proud you were or how they could have handled the situation better. You can use words like, '*When you do this …, I feel like this…*' Don't stress your child out by making everything a competition. No one likes to lose but being a gracious loser is just as important as being a gracious winner, if not more. Of course, don't go too far the other way and beat them at every game you play, this will just leave them feeling deflated and no good at anything.

Teach them that it's good to be proud when you do well at something, but not at the expense of another person's feelings. Model how to say something nice to the other player when they win or lose. Give them a nice bank of comments they can refer to when in these situations. Tell them that it's okay to be sad about losing but they should try to say something nice to the winner, as the winner shouldn't be made to feel bad as well, just for winning. Otherwise children will stop wanting to play with them if they are made to feel bad every time they win or lose. Keep the talk positive! I love when I'm playing games with my daughter and I lose, and she says to me, '*Good try mum*', it makes me very proud and so happy that this has sunk in with her. And as a pretty competitive person, I don't even mind losing when I hear this. Well not as much anyway.

It's sometimes hard as a parent to 'fake' interest in activities that your child likes to do, when you don't feel the same way. But it's important to engage with them in activities that they enjoy, even if you don't. It shows them that you're interested in them and care about things they do. Take time to just play with your child as well, with the only goal being to make happy memories together. Laugh, run, be silly, do whatever makes you smile, it will not only strengthen your relationship with each other but allow you to forget your worries for a bit. It's amazing how letting go of all your worries, even for just a few minutes, and having some carefree time with your child can really boost your attitude. It's a great stress reliever. It really gets those good endorphins going.

You can also work with your child to create something together. Maybe a picture, a collage, a building, whatever it may be, this can allow you to see how your child works with others. Are they a follower or a leader? Are they bossy and take over doing everything? Or are they lazy and want you to do all the work? It's also good to suggest ideas you know they won't like just to see how they will answer, as this is bound to happen when they're at school. They will be made to work in groups, sometimes with people they don't like or with people who have different opinions to them, and they will need to work it out, democratically and peacefully.

Friends

Helping them with their social skills before they get to school will help them develop good friendships at school. Friends can have a lot of influence over a child's emotional and mental health, so it is important for them to make the right friendships. You cannot be there with your child to handpick the friends you would like them to have, but you can certainly steer them in the right direction by giving them the skills to identify what makes a good friend and what does not. Every child, and adult for that matter, has a longing to belong, we all want to fit in and be a part of something. And sometimes we will do whatever we need to do to fit in, even if we know it's not the right thing to do.

Peer pressure and bullying are unfortunately still alive and well in schools, and they start from a very early age. It's important that your child knows about both, so they can identify when these things are happening to them. Peer pressure is when other children make you do something you may not really want to do or that you know you shouldn't do. And bullying is when a person repeatedly and intentionally uses words or actions to hurt you. A good anti-bullying website is www.bullyingnoway.gov.au. This website defines what bullying is, helps you to better understand it, teaches you how to respond to bullying and how to prevent it. It has games for children to learn about bullying, as well as puppets, activities and songs. It also has a free, interactive app that teaches your child about feelings, getting along and dealing with difficult situations in a fun way.

Acceptance and tolerance

Remember to talk to your child about acceptance and tolerance, how people are all different, in looks and abilities. But more importantly, model acceptance and tolerance in your own life. We all know children love to stare at anyone that's a bit different to them, whether they look different or they do things differently than they're used to. This is part of being a child. They don't know any better. But we need to teach them about people having different skin colours and speaking different languages. And that some people have physical disabilities and may not be able to see, hear, walk or talk. Teach them that some people will be tall, some will be short, and some will be small, and some will be big. They need to know that every child is different, just like every adult is different, and that it's okay to be different. How boring our world would be if we all looked and sounded the same?

Talk to your child about the fact that other children will be good at different things in their class. Some children will be good at some things, many things or a few things, like reading, writing, drawing, speaking, running, skipping or jumping. And that it's not okay to tease anyone who cannot do something, especially when they're having-a-go. Remember to teach them that not everything is a competition and they don't always have to be the first or the best at something. And the fact that they're at school to learn and that all children learn in a different way and at different times. Also, that something they find easy to do may be quite hard for another child to do, and vice versa.

Chapter 7
Don't Worry, Be Happy

Feelings

Your child's emotional development is just as important as their mental, physical and social development. If you want a happy child, you need to make sure they are emotionally secure. *'Either we spend time meeting children's emotional needs by filling their cup with love, or we spend time dealing with behaviours caused from their unmet needs. Either way, we spend the time.'* Pam Leo. When you acknowledge and accept their feelings, they feel relieved, they are probably thinking to themselves, *'I feel better, you understand me, maybe it's not so bad after all.'* You need to respect their feelings, all of their feelings, the good and the bad, even if they seem irrational to you. If they say they are scared of monsters, don't dismiss this emotion by telling them, *'Don't be silly. There's no such thing as monsters.'* Discuss this feeling of being scared with them. To them, at that point in time, monsters are a very real thing, they are scary, and they are probably keeping them up at night or giving them nightmares. This may be a real fear that they need to work through. And the fact that they're telling you, they may be asking for your help to understand this feeling.

Help your child to express their feelings with words. They may not have a huge vocabulary of emotions to use, so instead of correcting them or denying their feelings, when they have a negative feeling, think about the emotion they might be feeling, name it and put it in to a sentence. For example, when they say, *'I hate you. You never let me watch my shows.'* Instead of saying, *'No you don't, and you always get to watch your shows.*' Give them some better vocabulary than 'hate'. Try this instead, '*Sounds like you're sad that you didn't get to watch your show.*' This is helping them to name the feeling they may be really having, 'sad' instead of 'hate'. And this way they can better match their feelings to names and begin to use them more accurately. There's no need to lecture them, question them or even get angry when they are expressing their negative emotions. Simply help them to understand these strong emotions better. Begin using basic feeling words like sad, mad and scared to name their emotions. Over time they will begin to name their own emotions correctly and as they understand their emotions better you can teach them more sophisticated words like disappointed, frustrated and worried.

An important point to make with the scenario in the last paragraph, is that after stating, '*Sounds like you're sad that you didn't get to watch your show*', make sure you don't then give in and let them watch their show. If you have said no, stick with your decision. By stating the above, you are merely showing them that you accept how they're feeling. They're allowed to have feelings. You are giving your child the vocabulary they need to better express how they are feeling. All feelings need to be accepted but it's the negative actions that need to be addressed. For example, '*It's okay to be angry, but it's not okay to hit someone.*' When your child is having a big emotion sometimes it's hard for them to get over it, but you are there to help them get through it.

As a parent, we want to protect our children from sad emotions and discourage angry emotions. Even though we don't want to give attention to negative emotions, we still need to acknowledge them. This is very different to giving in to them. Don't forget to model describing how *you* feel to your child, they need to know that negative feelings are normal and that you too get angry, frustrated and annoyed at times, and not always at them. You are not a robot. You too have emotions, just like them. It's important that you own your emotions and phrase it as, *'I am upset.'* Be careful not to put it back on your child by saying, *'You made me upset'*, as they will just do the same to you. Get into the habit of replacing 'you' with 'I'. Instead of saying, *'You need to listen'*, you would start with *'I want you to listen because…'* By using 'you', your child might also get defensive. Instead of saying, *'You made a mess'*, try, *'Look at this mess.'* This way you're just stating the obvious, you're not getting into the 'blame game'. There are no winners in the blame game.

Children need positive strategies to deal with feelings of embarrassment, sadness and anger. Obviously, it's not nice when your child is embarrassed, sad or angry, but these are all emotions they will feel. They are big emotions that can be hard for little people to understand. You need to acknowledge and respect the emotion they are having and allow them to express themselves in a way that is appropriate. For instance, when your child is mad you can say to them, *'I know you're angry about… maybe you need some time to cool off before we talk about it.*' They may just need some time to run around and yell outside to expel some built up energy and frustration, go into their room and yell into their pillow or listen to some quiet music.

You will come to know your child, what they need and what works best to calm them down. But it's important that you talk about these 'big' feelings with your child, name them and show them how to deal with them. Talk about your own bad social experiences, and times when you've had bad feelings with your child, so they can see they're not alone and these things happen to everyone. And often we learn from these bad times and become a better person, and then again sometimes we don't, and that's just life.

Feelings about starting school

If your child is a bit anxious about starting school begin talking about school early. Keep the talk about school positive and fun. Talk about new concepts at school, like uniforms, teachers, show and tell, even the school bell. There are a lot of good picture books on starting school that you can read with your child and discuss. I have a list on my website for you to check out. You can even include school talk in their play, and role play being teachers and students during pretend play. This is a good way to practise sitting on the floor and listening. Talk about your own experiences of school, if they are positive ones. Some schools provide a transition program which is a bonus if you have an anxious child or even if you are a bit anxious about them starting school yourself. It allows your child to spend some time in the school environment with and without you before they begin the school year.

The transition program should include some information sessions for the parents that allow you to learn more about the school, what your child will be learning, how you can help them and give you a chance to voice any concerns you may have. And while you are at a parent information session your child might participate in some fun activities and get to know the other children who will become their future classmates. This way you both know what school is all about, have had a bit of a trial and it's not something unknown and scary any more. Your child will get to meet the teachers at the school and see what the classrooms are like. This can be the beginning of new relationships between your child, their teachers and peers, as well as for you with the teachers and other parents.

Temperaments

We are all born with different temperaments and we have them for life. Sometimes called our personality, but our temperament is how we respond to situations and people. It includes how we react emotionally, how we regulate our behaviour and how we respond to new situations. Your child may have a similar temperament to yourself or a very different one. Either way, our temperaments have a lot to do with how we deal with many social situations, as well as how we deal with each other at home. Some children, and adults, react very strongly to things, they may get very excited about fun events or very angry when things don't go their way. Just like some people may be able to control their behaviour and their feelings and others can have big tantrums. And some people are very sociable and handle meeting new people and being in new situations very well, and for others these events make them very nervous.

You can't change your temperament, but if you are aware of your own and your child's, this will help you to understand why you both react and behave the way you do. And if things are not going well between you and your child, you need to change how you react to them, you need to find strategies that work for you both. Even though you can't change your temperament, being aware of it, you can change your behaviour. And when your behaviour changes, so too will your child's. Life is tough. It's not a matter of if it will be tough, it's when. And how you and your child react when things get tough, shows a lot more about our character, than when things are good. Teach them to be responsible for their actions. Own what they've done and do the right thing to make it better.

Tantrums

Before I had children, I used to judge parents of children having tantrums in shopping centres. I would think to myself, *'Control your child, who's the parent here?'* I hate my naive, pre-child self for this. If only I knew what I know now, I would walk over and give those parents a high five, a hug or at least an understanding nod. And yes, while there are some pretty bad parents out there who couldn't care less about what their children do and say, there are a lot of parents trying their best. Unfortunately, children will be children, and sometimes their emotions get the better of them and this emotion overload comes out as a big ol' tantrum. And children aren't partial to where this happens. You could be in library, on a plane, in a waiting room or anywhere people are trying to be quiet, and bam! Tantrum time. This is when your parent survival skills and your fight or flight response kicks in. But it is important to remember this quote by L. R. Knost *'When little people are overwhelmed by big emotions, it's our job to share our calm, not to join their chaos.'*

I know it will be the last emotion you feel like having when your child is mid-meltdown, but you need to be calm. This applies to all conflict scenarios with your child, no matter how old they are. Whether they are two years old and rolling around on the floor or 12 years old and answering you back. You are the adult. You need to stay calm and get them through this, alive. Every child reacts differently when things don't go their way. Your child may yell, cry, run, sulk or get physical. You need to have some tricks up your sleeve to diffuse the situation and know what works for them. It may be that you both just need some time to calm down. You may both need a time-out from each other. But it's important to sort out the conflict when everyone's emotions are back to normal.

There's no point trying to talk things through mid-conflict as your child will not be listening and you will probably both say things you will later regret. You may need to leave the scene of the chaos, if this is appropriate to do so, until everyone calms down. If rules have been broken, don't forget to enforce relevant consequences. Being consistent is necessary so that your child learns that aggressive and disrespectful behaviour will not be tolerated. If your child breaks the rules, follow through with an appropriate consequence, every time.

Calming down

Ideally you want your child to be able to self-regulate their emotions, to control their impulses and be able to settle themselves. You can teach your child what to do when they begin to feel angry or upset. Having a time-out is just one way to calm them down. They could even get into the habit of putting themselves in a time-out when they're upset before they make a bad choice. This could be just going to their bedroom for a bit to calm down. If an activity is making them angry, move them to another calmer activity like drawing, colouring, doing a puzzle or looking at books.

Discuss with your child the signs to look out for when they're getting angry. They will be able to tell you most of these, like heart beating faster, making a fist with their hands, stomping their feet, wanting to yell or cry or both. Once they can recognise what their warning signs are, they are on their way to learning how to self-regulate. In the meantime, you may need to help them to settle down after big emotions. It helps if you model ways to calm down and practise these with them. This will give them a bank of strategies to use when the poop hits the fan. Other strategies to help your child (and yourself) calm down include:

- Take 10 slow, deep breaths
- Count to 10 slowly
- Go for a walk or run
- Listen to music
- Leave the situation
- Go outside
- Have a small snack
- Have a drink of water
- Lie down and close your eyes
- Hug a pillow or soft toy
- Count as high as you can
- Sing a song (e.g. Alphabet song)
- Scribble on some paper with crayons

- The Balloon: hold your hands in front of your mouth pretending to hold a small balloon. Pretend to blow up the balloon. As you blow, spread your hands apart to pretend the balloon is getting bigger. Once the balloon is as big as it can get, clap your hands together to 'pop' the balloon.

- The Pretzel: Sit down, cross your legs together and fold your arms across your chest like you're hugging yourself. Then squeeze yourself hard.

Effort and praise

As a parent you need to be positive towards your child's abilities, but don't be fake about it. Don't go over the top with your praise to the point that it's superficial. Of course, give them praise when they deserve it, just not all the time or it won't mean anything. And it will give your child an unrealistic idea of themselves and their abilities. They will think they are good at everything and when reality hits and they suddenly realise they are not the best at everything, it may come as a harsh reality. It's always a good idea to focus on praising the effort rather than the achievement. When you praise your child's effort and what they have done, more than the final outcome or product, it is a lot more motivational for them. When giving your child praise, use descriptive praise by stating exactly what you see. For instance, *'Thanks, you put all the books back on the shelf'* or *'You practised a lot to be able to ride your bike by yourself.'*

Avoid superlatives, like excellent, wonderful, clever and good. They are often used as, *'Good girl for cleaning up'* or *'Great work'* or *'You're so clever.'* These are too vague, and your child doesn't know what it is that they need to do next time to be successful again. And if it feels as though you are constantly telling your child to stop doing the wrong thing, stop! Wait until they do the slightest good thing and give them some descriptive praise for that. You always want to focus on the good behaviour rather than the bad as this is what you want to see repeated from your child. It's called 'catch them being good.' For instance, *'I like how quiet you are being in the car'* or *'You are sitting so nicely at the table eating breakfast.'* Even if they have only just started doing it, get in there before any negative behaviour has a chance to start. We want to give them attention for doing the right thing, not the wrong.

Growth mindset

You want to develop a 'growth mindset' in your child. This will help them to overcome challenges and setbacks they will be faced with. Children with a growth mindset believe their abilities can improve with time and effort. This is the opposite to a 'fixed mindset' where children believe their abilities are fixed and often give up on things rather than persevere with them. Children can swap between the two mindsets depending on the situation, but it's obviously the growth mindset that you want to encourage so it becomes habit. Teach your child that even though they may have failed on their first attempt at something, by having another try at it, they may succeed. Sometimes it's not just a matter of telling your child to try harder but getting them to try things in different ways that work for them.

Children need to understand that their brains can grow stronger with effort and time. That people aren't just born 'smart' or 'dumb', but they can do things to improve their knowledge and abilities. And that a lack of success just means they need to work harder. Children with a growth mindset love a challenge, seeing it as a way to improve and grow. They are more likely to ask for help when needed, and this is so important when they get to school. That instead of pretending they know what to do, copying other's work or hiding their mistakes from teachers, they get the help that they need to succeed. Get into the habit of when your child says, '*I can't do it*' or similar, simply add in '*yet.*' And get them to repeat it, so they are saying, '*I can't do it, yet.*' Say it all the time and soon enough it becomes their positive self-talk.

Resilience

If you can teach your child anything before they get to school, teach them to be resilient. School, like life, is not always fair. They will encounter many situations where they will need resilience to get through it. Their feelings will be hurt, other children will be mean to them and sometimes even adults will not be very nice. The best skill you can teach them is to 'bounce back'. This idea of 'bouncing back' means not letting the bad things get them down, or least when they do have bad feelings, they are able to get over them quickly. It's about adapting to bad situations, being able to forgive others and move on. It's about not letting them wallow in their sadness, but, to put it bluntly, to 'suck it up.' To young children everything is a catastrophe. *'I can't find my hat'*, catastrophe! *'You left the crust on my sandwich'*, catastrophe! *'I didn't get a turn on the ride'*, the world is ending! Now you can't change these things from happening, but you can teach your child how to bounce back from these so called 'tragedies'. And if they learn how to bounce back as a child, this will be an important skill they take with them into adulthood when things might actually be bad.

Catastrophe measure

A good concept to teach your child about resilience is the idea of a 'catastrophe measure', with 0 being 'nothing' to 10 being, you guessed it, 'a catastrophe'. You can make a vertical catastrophe measure using paper, put 0 at the bottom and number up to 10 at the top. Then to put things into perspective give them examples to number. For instance, *'You fell over and grazed your knee'*, discuss with them how that would make them feel, how long they would feel that way, and what number they would give it on the catastrophe measure. Now using this grazed knee as an example, it may get a 2 on the scale, depending on your child's pain tolerance. They might initially say it's a 10 and give answers like, it really hurts, it's so bad, it could be bleeding… but after discussing with you how there are a lot worse things that can happen and how people survive a grazed knee, as they probably already have, they should come to see that it's really not that bad. Whereas you might give them the example as the world ending being a 10 and compare this to grazing your knee. Always acknowledge their feelings and ideas of course but help them to put things into perspective. A grazed knee is literally not the end of the world.

Positive attitude

You want your child to be happy. This means they need to have a positive attitude. A child with a positive attitude has enthusiasm, motivation, cooperation, curiosity, confidence, self-reliance, impulse control, patience, perseverance, consideration and they are doing their best. And if you are not seeing these traits in your child, then here are some things to encourage them… Children are naturally curious about their world, so this is an easy one to encourage. Let them explore and work out things for themselves, as long as it is safe to do so. When they want to know about things, teach them or teach yourself first, and then teach them. Stand back and let your child do things for themselves, have-a-go, try new things and don't give up when things get tricky. This is an easy way to encourage their confidence, self-reliance and perseverance.

PREPPING FOR SCHOOL SUCCESS

Even when there are things they don't want to be doing or they find boring, get them to do them anyway, this teaches them motivation. Motivation is all about 'working tough', doing things that need to be done, whether they are fun or not. Don't jump at their every beck and call, acknowledge them and let them know when you can join or help them. It's okay for them to wait as this teaches them patience and impulse control. A great skill to have when there are 25 or so children wanting a turn, or the teachers help. Get excited about things and enjoy their excitement at the little things in life. Laugh, be silly, have fun! This encourages their enthusiasm. And give them time to play with other children, this is an easy way to teach them how to cooperate with others. Young children often want to do their own thing in their own time, so learning how to play with others and think about others' wants and feelings not only helps with cooperation but consideration.

Cooperation is a big one. Especially when it comes to having a well-behaved and happy child. Ideally you want your child to do what they are told, when they are told, without any drama. And until your child can cooperate with you, trying to teach them any other skills is pointless. When they cooperate it's a beautiful thing. And the benefit is that we get less resistance from them, which gives us more time, happiness and affection. Which in turn makes us confident parents with confident children. On the negative side, when there is a lack of cooperation we get: nagging, arguments, tantrums, yelling, frustration, stress, negotiating… all that fun stuff!

Once your child is cooperating with you, you can teach them to be more self-reliant. This means getting them to do things that they are capable of for themselves. This gives them confidence as they are using their own strengths to improve their weaknesses. And as a bonus you should get more time to do other things. When we do things for our child that they are capable of doing, we take away the chance for them to be self-reliant and confident. It also tells them that we think they can't do it, or they don't need to do it. Remember you are not a slave, no matter what you're currently doing for your child, think to yourself, *'What part of this could they do themselves?'* By doing this you are giving them more skills than doing it for them. These qualities will help your child to succeed, not only at school but in life.

Social-Emotional Learning (SEL)

Schools, good schools, focus on teaching the whole child. They realise that schools are not just where children develop academically, but socially, emotionally and physically as well. And if they go to a religious school, you can add spiritually to that list. They teach children the skills they need to thrive. Schools have Social-Emotional Learning (SEL) programs to help your child. Research shows that children who participate in SEL programs have better academic success, positive attitudes and behaviours. These programs not only help your child succeed at school, but throughout their lives. Through these programs your child will learn confidence, organisation, persistence, resilience and getting along skills. As well as goal setting, decision making, problem solving, calming down and collaboration skills. Children learn to manage their own feelings and behaviours, show empathy and compassion for others, be assertive, control their impulses and maintain healthy relationships.

It's important to note that children who are socially and emotionally confident have more friends, feel like they belong and are less bullied. In the early years these programs can focus on skills such as listening, managing behaviours, getting along with others and paying attention to help them succeed at school. And it's often these skills that early childhood teachers see as more important than other academic skills. As until children can listen, pay attention and behave, it's hard to teach them anything.

If you are already noticing that your child has some social-emotional issues, or you just want to get a head start on their social-emotional learning, some areas for you to work on with your child include:

- Listening and paying attention – full body listening with looking eyes, listening ears, lips locked, still body

- Speaking to others – using greetings, being welcoming, using manners

- Following directions – doing things step-by-step, repeating things to remember them

- Self-talk – using positive words, saying things quietly or inside your head

- Being assertive – getting your needs met, speaking up, questioning, looking at the person, using a respectful voice

- Identifying feelings – naming feelings, strong feelings, identifying what feelings do inside our bodies, recognising other's feelings by their face and body clues, having different feelings about the same thing, calming down

- Helping others – noticing when others need help, caring for others

- Dealing with accidents – what to do and how to get help, difference between accidents and doing things on purpose, checking if others are okay even when it's an accident

- Playing nicely – how to play together, take turns, share, be fair, have fun, join in, invite others

- Problem solving – naming the problem, thinking of solutions

- Making friends – how to be a friend, be kind, make new friends, keep friends

- Being organised – packing away toys, cleaning their room, getting ready in the morning, following a visual routine

- Being persistent – finishing things that you start

- Getting along – respecting and accepting other people

- Being confident – asking for help when needed, doing things on their own, trying new things

- Being resilient – showing self-control, accepting consequences for their actions

Bucket Fillers

Think of yourself and your child as 'bucket fillers'. With the 'bucket' being our emotional and mental wellbeing, it holds our good thoughts and feelings about ourselves. We want to make sure we are filling up others' buckets with positive words and actions, being a 'bucket filler'. This makes us, and others feel happy and good. We don't want to be dipping into others' buckets with our negative words and actions. This empties others' buckets, making them feel sad and it makes us a 'bucket dipper'. We need to fill our child's bucket with love, affection, security and attention because in years from now they won't remember what we said to them but how we made them feel. Check out the picture books, *'Have You Filled a Bucket Today? A Guide to Daily Happiness for Kids'* by Carol McCloud and *'How Full Is Your Bucket? For Kids'* by Tom Rath and Mary Reckmeyer, for more on the concept of being a bucket filler. It's a nice way for children to understand how their words and actions affect others, both positively and negatively.

Chapter 8
Oh Behave

Behaviour

When children don't feel right, they can't behave right. When they are not behaving as they should you first need to rule out whether they may just be tired or hungry. Until these issues are dealt with there's no point in trying to sort out any other behaviour issues. If your child is making bad choices, sometimes they just need to be redirected to a new activity to distract them. It's almost like showing them something shiny to distract them. It can be as simple as a change of environment to change their mood. When you are talking to them about their behaviour, make sure you concentrate on their behaviour and not them as a person. Keep talk with your child positive, firm and consistent. Instead of saying, *'You are being naughty'*, you say, *'When you threw the crayons all over the floor, that was wrong.'* This way we are not saying they are a bad child, but the behaviour that they just did was bad. Remember that our words become their inner voice. We don't want our child to think of themselves as naughty and bad. We want them to always feel accepted and that our love for them is unconditional.

I sometimes find myself saying to my daughter, *'I love you, but I do not love your behaviour or what you're doing right now.'* If your child is doing something that is unsafe, and you stop them, make sure they understand that you are doing what you're doing to protect them, not punish them. Your child may feel like you have so many rules about everything but remind them that you are not there to be the 'fun police' or their friend, but to keep them safe and teach them right from wrong. And although it may be fun to run around in the house or jump on the lounge, it's not safe.

Time-out

Love them or hate them time-outs are still pretty effective and widely used in schools. Call it what you like but removing your child when they are misbehaving, from an interesting activity and your attention, to another location for a set amount of time is a time-out. If you are at home, it might be a corner that is free from distractions and if you are out it may be sitting them with you. The idea of a time-out is pretty self-explanatory, it gives your child some time to calm down and change their behaviour. Word of warning though, it may initially make them even worse. Persevere. The important thing is that you are not giving them your attention. A rule of thumb is that the time-out should match their age in minutes, e.g. 3 minutes for a 3-year-old. It can be helpful to use a timer. Only start the timer when they are in the time out area and if they need to be placed back in the time-out area, the timer starts again.

Some children are more strong-willed than others. But it's a good habit to get into as it will probably be one your school uses. Often in class there are a lot of things going on and when things go wrong it's helpful for the child and the teacher to have some cool off time before dealing with a situation.

Obviously depending on the severity of the situation it may not be the best choice. But it works well for misbehaviour as it removes the child from whatever the problem is, it gives them time to calm down and think about what they've done. It also gets them away from any other children that may be the problem and gives the teacher time to sort it out better than being in the heat of the moment. It's important that after a time-out you get your child to answer the following questions:

- What did you do?
- Why was it wrong? (if they were in the wrong)
- What should you have done?
- How will you make things better?
- What will you do next time?

It is a lot more effective when these answers come from them. This way they are owning their choices, and this is better than you giving them a lecture on all of the above points. Children are pretty good at tuning out when you start lecturing them about their behaviour. I have provided a 'Think sheet' on my website for you to refer to. Time-outs should be used sparingly and as just one of your many parenting techniques. They are a non-harmful way to help your child regulate their own emotions and behaviour.

'My child wouldn't do that'

Every parent thinks their child is perfect. I'm going to let you in on a little teacher secret here… they're not. No child is perfect, not yours, the one you see sitting quietly at the café sipping their babycino or anyone's. Children will be children. And while yes, there are very good children, none are perfect. Please remember this when your child's teacher is telling you something wrong they have done in class and all you can think is there's no way my child would do that! If the teacher is telling you that your child did something, believe them! Teachers are not out to get you or your child. Teachers actually love children and want the best for them. Just like you want the best for your child. Sometimes it can be hard to hear that your perfect angel is not so perfect but please don't be in denial. This helps no one. Work out why they are doing the things they're doing so it can be fixed.

Please don't be the ostrich parent with your head in the sand ignoring any negatives said about your child. Be proactive and work out what you can do to help them. There needs to be a good relationship between the school and the home for your child to succeed. Your child needs to see their parents and teachers communicating positively and sharing a common goal… to help them succeed. Never speak about the teachers negatively in front of your child, this harms the relationship. It is hard to form a positive relationship when there is no respect for one another, this includes parents, teachers and children.

School rules

You are your child's first teacher remember, teach them to respect the rules that their school has. The rules are there for a reason! They may seem trivial to you and mere recommendations, but they have been important enough to write down, the least you can do is follow them. Get your child off to a good start by helping them fit in, not stand out. Everything is new to them, they need your help, your guidance, they are taking your lead, lead them in the right direction. Explain to them why they are doing these things, so they too can see reason behind them. We all know children love to ask why, give them the why, then they can see why they need to follow the rules in the first place. And if you don't know the why, ask or make up a good reason for them, parents are great at this, this thinking on the spot, telling little white lies, just don't go with, *'Because I said so,'* like I sometimes got as a child, this is helpful to no one.

Rules & Consequences

Sometimes it's hard to be the happy, easy-going parent who is 'cool' about everything. We often turn into nagging, yelling, crazy people who no one listens to. And why? Well probably because we say the same things every day, numerous times a day. Who wouldn't be driven crazy by this? Children are often off in their own little worlds and then you come along with all your rules and expectations, seemingly to spoil all their fun. I find most children are very good at tuning out their parents' voices. It's almost as if their parent starts talking and a little switch goes off in their brain saying, *'blah, blah, blah'* over whatever their parents are saying to them. Or often we are trying to tell them things when they are in the middle of doing something else. Now we know how annoying this is when it is done to us, but for some reason we do it to our children and expect them to listen. A good tactic is to always gain your child's attention, and their eye contact before you talk to them, otherwise you are just wasting your breath! They are probably half listening or not listening at all, and this is where the repeating, nagging and yelling starts.

Children need rules and consequences to feel secure in their environment. They need to know that there are always consequences for their actions. As a parent, you need to be consistent in your approach to discipline. It's more the certainty that there will be a consequence, rather than the severity of the consequence. And all parents need to be on the same page when it comes to discipline. It's impossible to agree on everything, but you need to have each other's back when it comes to family values and discipline. This is the only way it will work. Otherwise it's confusing for the child and you both, there's no consistency and they don't know where they stand and what's going to happen following their actions. There shouldn't be a 'good cop/bad cop' scenario happening in your home, you need to be both, maybe multiple times a day. It's not fair for one parent to be the 'good cop' all the time, dishing out all the rewards, fun, hugs and yes's… while the other parent is stuck being the 'bad cop', giving all the time-outs, warnings and no's.

Remember you do need to be reasonable as a parent. Often you will need to just go with your heart, your instinct and do the best you can do with what you have. Every parent and child are different, and you need to work out what it best for your family. And, at the end of the day, you are there to love and take care of your child, preparing them to be good, well-adjusted people, and this is no small task, it's a balancing act, and requires everyone doing their share.

You need to know your child's 'currency', this is not money but the things they value. Your child's currency may be an item or an activity that they value. It will be different for each child, but it could be simple things like an extra story or song at bedtime, extra play or screen time, some messy play, an outing, a board game, choosing a special meal, having a picnic, or sleeping in a different place. You can use their currency as a motivation for positive behaviour, and if necessary, as a punishment for negative behaviour. It is best to use it as an incentive, as you should be focusing on their positive behaviours. But when negative behaviours arise, removing their currency for a set period of time is something that they will respond to.

Make sure you give your child options, so they feel like they have a choice and a say in matters. You can't be a dictator, telling them everything they need to do, say, wear and eat. They have their own minds too and want to feel that they have been heard and their opinions matter. Even if you narrow their options down to two that you've pre-selected, they will still feel as though they've had a choice about something. It may be as simple as choosing their clothes, lunch, a book to read... anything... let them have a say about things. This should avoid a lot of conflict.

Children need to know that every choice they make has a consequence. Yes 'consequence' is a big word to say, but just explain it to them so they understand it, before you use it. For example, you hit your brother, that was your choice, you chose to do that, and because of that bad choice you made, you now must have some time out, that is your consequence. It might not come out like that, in the heat of the moment, so you can always wait until you've both calmed down to explain what the bad choice was and what the negative consequence was. Don't forget to use the word 'consequence' as a positive too. For example, *'You packed up your toys without being asked, thank you, as a consequence let's play that game you wanted to play.'* It is important that consequences are consistent, age appropriate, relevant to the action and meaningful to the child. Another important thing to teach your child about consequences, is accepting them. If you have told them to sit in the corner for a time-out as a consequence, they need to sit in the corner, without screaming, saying no or just flat out refusing to. This will take practise to perfect. Consistency on your part is key, so that the consequences you are using become routine. This is no walk in the park.

Discipline

It's important to teach your child right from wrong and provide them with boundaries from a young age. This is not something to leave up to the school. We all know that children love to test boundaries and they are often just doing this to understand where they stand. Again, you need to be consistent. Children thrive in environments that are consistent, safe and loving. People often talk about 'discipline' and 'punishment' when teaching children right from wrong. These words have such negative connotations with them. We need to think about the origins of these words… 'discipline' from the Latin word 'disciplina' meaning *'to teach, to learn'* and punish from the Latin word 'punire' meaning *'to cause pain for an offense.'* I think discipline is effective, but punishment is not. You need to be thinking as a parent, *'Do I want to hurt or help my child?'* With surely the answer being you want to help them. Nothing good comes from hurting them.

The problem is that effective discipline takes time, whereas in the heat of the moment a punishment is the easy way out. Parents often punish when they're emotional, later regretting their decision. Discipline is something you need to do when you're not emotional. Parents need to be on the same page when it comes to discipline. After an incident you can discuss with your partner, this is what happened, and this is what I did. It's then a good idea to discuss what should we do next time. When you are telling your child a rule, it always helps to tell them why. And no, *'Because I said so,'* is not a good reason why they should do something. For instance, when telling them to put their hat on, you could add, so you don't get sunburnt. Hopefully before they sneak in a long winded, *'Whyyyyyy?'* You also need to think about things from their perspective and give them responsibility to solve their own problems. Thinking about the above example from their perspective, they just want to get to the park and play, they're not thinking about their hat and being sun smart. But you can use a 'think aloud' saying, *'It's a sunny day, I wonder what we'll need at the park?'* to help them out.

Bullying and being mean

Don't wait for bullying to happen to talk about it with your child. Children need to know what bullying is, what to do if it happens to them and that they are not alone in dealing with it. They need to know that they can come to you, a teacher or another trusted adult if they are being bullied at school. Bullying is not just physical, like a child getting pushed around by another child. It can also be emotional, like a child being excluded by others in their class. Or verbal, like someone teasing and saying mean things to them. It may sound very stereotypical but it's often young boys who get into the physical or verbal bullying and young girls who do the emotional or verbal bullying. We've all met 'mean girls' before. They often have a little group of friends that think they're better than their peers and treat everyone else like they are less than them. They use phrases like, *'You're not invited to my party'*, *'If you don't… I'll tell on you'*, *'You're not my friend'*, and *'You can't play with us.'* As well as a lot of other 'nice' one-liners. They have often mastered the eye roll and the 'look you up and down'. They are sassy, feisty and just not very nice. They can also be very sneaky. Teachers and parents may think they are wonderful as they do all their 'mean' things away from adults, so they don't get caught.

You can use social stories with your child to act out bullying scenarios that they may encounter at school to prepare them on how to respond effectively. Once they can identify which children are 'bullies' by what they say and do to other children, they can better avoid them. Your child needs conflict resolution skills to deal with issues when they occur and resilience to help them 'get over it'. You don't want a playground issue getting out of hand and distracting them for the rest of the day and affecting their learning. Some 'bullies' have a lot of 'friends', I use the word 'friend' lightly as they are only 'friends' with them through fear of being bullied themselves. Don't forget to talk to your child about 'bystanders'. Bystanders are people, who as the name suggests, just stand by and let the bullying happen. They don't stand up for others that are being bullied. They simply watch and do nothing. This can be as bad as being the actual bully, as the bully only has 'power' when others are afraid of them. If, on the other hand, other people ignored and paid no attention to what the bully was doing or even better, stood up to them, they would lose their power.

Children can be cruel and often don't realise the effect this has on others. The old saying of, *'Sticks and stones may break my bones, but names can never hurt me'* is so far from the truth it's ridiculous. It really needs to be changed to, *'Sticks and stones will hurt my bones, just as much as words will.'* As a parent, you need to be aware of bullying and be proactive about it. Don't be in denial and think it won't happen to my child. Preparing them for it is the best thing you can do for them. There's no such thing as a 'bully-proof child', but you can surely give them the skills and strategies they need to survive.

Young children can often be unintentionally mean. They are merely trying to assert themselves and work out some sort of pecking order between their peers. Not to say that this still doesn't hurt others, but that they need to be taught that what they're doing or saying hurts others. You can't assume that young children are being mean on purpose, just to hurt others. Children are egocentric, and the thought of other's feelings doesn't come until they are older. They think about themselves and getting their needs and wants met, no matter how this affects others.

Friend or foe?

Children also need to understand that friendships change over time as they change; and that this is okay, and that the friends that they have when they are young may not be the friends they have when they're older. Their friendship groups will change as they change from Kindy to Prep, Prep to Year 1 and again as they become interested in different things, play different sports or move to different schools. You may need to prepare your child for this and encourage them to have friends from different friendship circles. They may have school friends, neighbourhood friends, team mates, family friends, and more. It is important for your child not to be so attached to just one friend that they can't function without them. It's cute to have a BFF (Best Friend Forever), but not if that's their one and only friend. Their BFF may have sick days from school, be in a different class, move to another school or simply find a new BFF. And then what? Your child will have no friends. It's best to encourage them to have a few different friends.

No child is immune to bullying and it can often happen from their 'friends' who may be their friends one day and not the next. This is not a friendship and your child needs to be able to recognise the signs of a good and bad friend, so they know who to consider as a real friend. Making new friends can be tricky. Play is a good way for your child to make new friends. You can watch how they play with others and see who they play nicely with and organise future play dates with them. These could then become your child's friends. You can organise play dates with your friends' children, other parents with children you meet at playgroups or in your neighbourhood. Make sure if you've had a play date at your house, you wait to be invited for a play date at their house before re-inviting them to yours. You don't want to be the only one interested in the friendship. It's a two-way street.

Talk with parents you meet to find out what school their child will be going to, then encourage future playdates with children who will be going to the same school as your child. You will work out pretty quickly which children they like to play with and who they get along with. As well as which children they don't. Some children just click and get along easily without adult intervention. These are the friendships you should encourage. You will need to teach your child friendship making skills like how to join in games, initiate play, not be excluded and how to include others. They need practise talking and listening to other children, as well as how to play nicely, so they get better at it. Make sure you provide them with lots of opportunities to socialise with other children before they begin school. Practise makes perfect! You also need to teach them that to have good friends, they need to be a good friend. They need to be kind, share, take turns, help others, act friendly and be interested in what other children are doing. Even young children can make small gifts, draw pictures, write letters to friends to show they care. This is a nice way to interact with your new friends.

There will be days at school when your child may be excluded by their peers and they will inevitably tell a teacher on duty, who will likely respond with, *'Go and find someone else to play with'* or *'Play something else.'* These responses obviously don't fix the problem of your child being excluded or having their feelings hurt. It brushes over the problem and offers an easy solution. Make sure when they are telling you the same thing after school, that you don't respond in the same way. They are obviously hurt by it and need to be heard. They want someone to understand how they feel and help them to find a solution, so it doesn't happen again. You need to be aware if this is a regular complaint, where your child is often upset after school and complaining that they have no one to play with. In this case, you may need to talk with their teacher to find out what is happening with them at play times. Who are they playing with or who could they be encouraged to play with.

If you child is not happy at school, it may be because they do not have any friends, or they are being bullied. If you have tried to sort out these problems and nothing changes, you may need to consider changing schools. Just make sure this is not your first option and you have tried other ways to improve their level of happiness at school first. And, make sure that it's the school and the children in the school that are the problem and not your child, as changing schools will not help if the problem is your child.

Making amends

Make sure if your child has done the wrong thing, especially to another child, they do something to make it better. You may decide on an appropriate consequence to give them. And this is fine, but by simply punishing them all they feel is bad about themselves. Don't forget the next step and get them to make amends, to fix the problem. This makes them feel good about themselves. It allows your child to see themselves as a good person. And even though they may have done a bad thing, they are not a bad person. This is important for not only school but life. It teaches them to recognise what they have done wrong and to do something to make it better. It also teaches your child to be kind, honest and generous. By admitting they have done wrong (honesty), doing something to make the other person feel better (kindness) and doing it out of their own free will (generosity). Win, win, win!

Chapter 9
Let's Get Physical

By the time your child is starting school they have come such a long way from when they were a baby. Not only have they learnt a lot, but they can do a lot of things. This chapter is related to their physical development, coordinating their mind and body to complete tasks. It's about having a healthy body, being active and avoiding too much screen time. You are your child's best role model when it comes to them developing a healthy lifestyle. You need to lead by example by eating healthy, buying healthy foods, being active and providing your child with lots of opportunities to be active as well. Go for walks together, make healthy meals together, play at the park together, just move! Keep activities fun and inclusive for your child's age and stage of development. For instance, don't take your two-year-old on a long hike, unless you plan on carrying them most of the way. Children need opportunities to be active every day! Yep, every day!

Healthy eating

As a parent you need to provide your child with a balanced diet. They need to be exposed to many different foods and always be encouraged to try new foods. A rule in our house is that you can't say you don't like something if you haven't tried it yet. I like having food at other peoples' houses too, as I find it exposes my child to new foods that I don't like, so we don't have them at our house. For instance, my husband and I are not pawpaw fans, yet my daughter loves them. And I only found this out by her having some when she was at her Nanna's house. And another time she came home saying she likes squishy cow cheese after being at her Nanny Joan's house. After some investigation this turned out to be '*The Laughing Cow*' cheese, which is spreadable cheese that comes in little individually wrapped triangles (just so you know). Children need three meals (breakfast, lunch, dinner) a day and snacks (morning, afternoon), lots of snacks if your child is anything like mine. Children have small stomachs, so lots of small amounts of food throughout the day is better than three big meals.

The trick is to find healthy snacks and meals. It's so easy to buy junk food and fast food. But this is so bad for their (and your) bodies. They need quality, fresh foods to help their little bodies grow. The best foods are unprocessed foods, like fresh fruits and vegetables, dairy, meat and whole grains. And of course, home-cooked meals, where you know exactly what is in the food. Limit the amount of processed foods and foods with a lot of sugar, salt and fat they are having. When your child is thirsty, stick to water. Avoid too much juice, it may seem like a healthy alternative but it's a lot of sugar minus the fibre they get from actually eating a piece of fruit. Some experts warn that fruit juice contains just as much sugar as fizzy drinks. And try not to use dessert as a reward for eating their dinner or if you are having a dessert, make it fruit or yoghurt instead of ice-cream. Children's appetites can change from day to day, even meal to meal. Try not to force them to eat if they are not interested, they will be hungry next meal time.

Physical activity

Physical activity is important for your child's growing body. And as a bonus, when your child is doing a lot of physical activity they are healthier, fall asleep easier and sleep better as they're more tired. It can also be a good outlet for any negative emotions they may be feeling and help them improve their mood and self-esteem. It allows your child to use up any built-up energy they may have, and this is especially necessary after a day at school when they have spent a lot of time sitting, listening and being quiet. And even though it may mean being loud and running around, it's actually a good way to calm them down. It's important to develop a healthy, active lifestyle early in life for this to become a habit. Being active has been proven to help children do better at school, hence why I've included it in my book.

Physical activity gives your child a strong and healthy body. It is good for their heart, lungs, bones and muscles. It makes them more flexible, keeps them at a healthy weight and lowers their risk of health problems and diseases. They need a variety of activities from ones that make them sweat and puff, to ones that strengthen their bones and muscles. They might have some high-intensity activities like swimming and running fast or for a long time, some moderate-intensity activities like riding a bike or fast walking, and some activities like skipping or ball games that strengthen their body. By the time they start school your child should be doing at least one hour of physical activity a day. And of course, this includes all that energetic play they do!

Gross motor skills

Being active allows your child to develop their fine and gross motor skills. Firstly, their gross motor skills are the physical skills they are doing when they perform large body movements, usually using their whole hand, arm, foot and leg. These skills need to be practised from a young age, so their movements become accurate and fluent. It allows your child to develop good spatial and body awareness, strength, endurance, coordination, stability, balance, core strength and posture. And these skills are needed to complete physical activities successfully, without looking clumsy. Children use gross motor skills to perform many everyday tasks such as standing, sitting, walking, playing and taking care of themselves. There are lots of activities you can do with your child to improve and strengthen their gross motor skills, these include:

- Kicking, catching, throwing and bouncing balls
- Skipping and jumping
- Hopping on one foot and then the other
- Balancing on one foot and then the other (with eyes opened and closed)
- Running
- Marching (using their arms and legs)
- Moving forwards and backwards
- Walking heel-to-toe forwards and backwards
- Animal walking (bear walk, crab crawl, frog jump, bunny hop, etc.)

- Hopscotch (draw it on a footpath with chalk)
- Obstacle course (inside or outside, include different movements)
- Pop bubbles (alternating hands)
- Dancing (e.g. hockey pokey)
- Simon says (with different body movements)
- Twister
- Yoga (copying you, Yoga picture cards or Yoga videos for kids)
- Washing the car
- Going to a playground where they can run, swing, hang, climb, jump and balance

Fine motor skills

Fine motor skills are developed by manipulating small objects with your fingers. It is all about moving the small muscles in your hand, fingers and thumb in a precise and coordinated way. And just like developing your child's gross motor skills, practice makes perfect. It helps your child's accuracy, hand strength, pincer grasp, hand coordination and individual finger movements. Fine motor skills are used every day for things like dressing, eating, brushing teeth and hair, using utensils, playing and holding objects. They are important for school when your child is writing, drawing, cutting, gluing, painting, opening containers and playing. Children need to be specifically taught how to hold a pencil and scissors correctly. I've included the correct pencil grip and scissor grip on my website for you to refer to. Perfecting this comes with age and practise. You can encourage your child to hold these tools correctly and model to them the correct way to use them, but until they are physically able to, don't force them, it will come. There are many things you can do with your child to practise and strengthen their fine motor skills, including:

- Cutting along a straight line, curved line and corners (using right or left-handed child size scissors)
- Gluing (using glue sticks, brushes)
- Drawing and colouring with different tools (pencil, crayon, pen, chalk, pencil grip)
- Painting (brush, finger)
- Playdough (squeeze, roll, push, poke, use rollers, cutters, etc.)
- Construction activities (Lego, Duplo, blocks)
- Playing with tongs and tweezers to pick things up
- Using pegs (around the edge of containers)
- Threading beads and lacing cards
- Buttoning and zipping
- Opening and closing containers
- Folding paper
- Using stickers (peeling them off as well)
- Sharpening pencils
- Playing with finger puppets
- Playing board games, card games, puzzles, pick up sticks

- Sing songs with finger actions (*Incy Wincy Spider*, *Twinkle Twinkle Little Star*, etc.)
- Playing musical instruments (xylophone, recorder, guitar, etc.)
- Cooking (stirring, measuring, beating)
- Water plants with a spray bottle or water gun

Hand dominance (left or right handed)

If you observe your child, from around the age of two, you will notice them using one hand more than the other, this could become their preferred/dominant hand. It can be difficult though, as children between the ages of two and four often swap between their left and right hands, so it can be hard to work out which is their dominant hand. However, by the time your child is around the age of four their preference should be clear. Never force either side to be your child's dominant hand. You can get an idea of which side they prefer by placing objects, like a pencil, in front of them and to the centre, so they can choose which hand to grab it with. Once their dominant hand is established, then it's time to encourage them to consistently use this hand when cutting, drawing, etc. to help them perfect and strengthen their grip.

When drawing for example, the dominate hand is the hand that holds the pencil and the other hand holds the paper. You can refer to their dominant hand as their 'doing hand'

and the other hand as their 'helping hand'. If your child's hand becomes tired during an activity, get them to have a little rest (stretch/shake their hand), rather than letting them swap hands. They may need little breaks to rest their hand until it is strong enough to be used consistently.

Scissor grip

If you can teach them a good scissor grip before school this will benefit them greatly. Make sure your child has child-sized scissors and they are right- or left-handed ones, depending on their dominant had. Teach them to keep their thumb on top in the small scissor handle in the 'thumbs up' position, their middle finger (and if room their ring finger) in the larger scissor handle, with other fingers curled into the palm. Keep their elbow tucked in, cut in the direction going away from your body, scissors pointing straight ahead, move the paper not the scissors and to use their non-dominant hand for support and moving the paper. Don't forget to teach them how to be safe with scissors by holding them with the blades closed, gripping the blade end in their hand, forming a fist around the blade and just leaving the handle showing. Walk with scissors close to your side and never run with them. To practice using scissors you can get your child to cut up long pieces of playdough, snip paper into small pieces, cut along straight, zigzag and curved lines, around circles, spirals, corners and pictures.

Pencil grip

Children go through developmental phases when learning how to hold a pencil correctly. They will naturally develop a pencil grip that is comfortable for them. But if your child has an awkward grip when holding a pencil be careful that this doesn't become a habit, as it will then be more difficult to change when they're older. Encourage your child to hold their pencil in a way that allows them to move their hand and fingers freely and easily when using it on paper. Teach them to hold a pencil between their thumb, index and middle fingers, with all three finger tips joining together, with the ring and little fingers bent and resting on the table, wrist slightly bent back and forearm resting on the table. Hold the pencil about 1-2cm from the tip. Model the correct grip for them and help them to place their fingers in the correct position.

Show them how to sit in a chair in a good sitting position. This is where their bottom is to the back of the chair, back up straight, feet flat on the floor and forearms resting on the table. Make sure your child has a chair and table suitable for their height to achieve this correct sitting position. You can even say a chant to help them remember, *'1, 2, 3, 4… Are your feet flat on the floor? 5, 6, 7, 8… Is your back up nice and straight? 9, 10, 11, 12… Show me how your pencil's held.'* If they need extra help keeping their fingers in the correct position on their pencil, you can always buy them a rubber pencil grip. There are many different styles available, but they are not to be used as a substitute to working on their fine motor skills. The rubber grip will not strengthen their grip or improve their fine motor skills, but it will help their finger position and may make it more comfortable for them. There are phases that your child will go through in learning how to hold a pencil correctly. These are on my website.

Crossing the midline

If you imagine a line running vertically down the middle of your body, this is your midline and it divides your body into left and right sides. Now 'crossing the midline' is all about using your arms or legs to reach across this line. Now why is this important? Your child's ability to cross over their midline effectively, helps them to strengthen their dominant hand and perform other school activities. Activities such as sitting cross-legged, putting on socks and shoes with both hands, writing across a piece of paper, reading from left to right and hand-eye coordination in sports.

A lot of the fine motor activities previously listed will give your child practice at crossing their midline. Activities like cutting, threading beads, buttoning, marching and playing Twister and Simon Says. Putting stickers on one of their arms and getting them to remove them with the opposite hand is a fun one to try. Even just getting them to copy you doing some body movements where you are consciously crossing over your midline. For example, touching your right shoulder with your left hand, and vice versa, bending over and touching your left foot with your right hand, and vice versa. I think you get the idea…

Screen time

The biggest way to get your child to be more active is to limit their screen time. And by screen time I mean time spent in front of tablets, television, smart phones, computers and video games. The World Health Organisation (WHO) recommends that children under the age of two should have no screen time at all. And children aged two to four years old should have less that one hour of screen time per day. Good luck with this… Everything in moderation I say. Yes, they should not be staring at screens too much I agree, but your child could have no screen time all week and then watch a movie, that will be longer than one hour, on the weekend. You're not exactly going to stop it at one hour and say no more until tomorrow. Plus, there are a lot of educational programs and games on screens and some will even be set as homework by your child's school.

In relation to screen time, as a parent you need to be mindful of what you are watching when your child is around. Is it something you want them exposed to at this age? Do you want to have to answer all the awkward questions about it later? If not, then best to change the channel to something more child friendly or turn it off. Screens are great when used appropriately. Obviously if your child is using them to watch educational shows or play educational apps, this would be ideal. But they are going to want to watch 'rubbish' shows and play 'mind-numbing' apps given the opportunity. And this is fine in moderation. A word of warning though… children who watch programs that encourage imagination and getting along are more likely to mimic these traits. And children who watch shows with violent and rude characters are more likely to mimic these undesirable behaviours. We all need 'downtime' when we can allow our brains to switch off and relax for a bit. Take note of the 'for a bit' part as you don't want them turning into zombies staring at their screens for hours on end. Some of the shows and apps can be very addictive and that's the last thing you need, your child addicted to watching or playing screens. You need to monitor your child's screen time, too much is not good for their growing brains. It's important to limit the time they have on screens as it replaces fundamental developmental skills they need to be learning in the limited time they are awake.

As a parent you need to be sure that what your child is watching or playing is safe. Our world, unfortunately, is full of weirdos, and no matter how hard we try to protect our children from them, there are many ways they can get to our children, and via the Internet is a big one. But it's also one way that thankfully you can be proactive in stopping them. For instance, only let your child watch clips on

'YouTube Kids' not 'YouTube' or set restrictions up on their devices that only allows them to view 'G rated' or 'PG rated' material. You can also set up timers that turn the Internet or certain apps off at certain times on their devices, so they are not watching their screens at inappropriate times. Find out how you can monitor or filter what your child is watching and only allow them to use screens where you can see what they're watching.

If your child wants to watch things on YouTube put it on the TV where everyone can see it, as even when you put restrictions on, inappropriate previews and ads still get through. Think about the context, the content and the child when using screen time. Firstly, the context, as in what else should they be doing right now? Talking with visitors, doing their chores, eating a meal? Think about whether it is an appropriate time for screens. Next, the content, what are they watching? Is it worthwhile or rubbish? And of course, the child, what is best for my child right now? This can depend on their age, their abilities and their interests.

You need to trust your child, but also monitor them. You can also pay to have programs that allow you to manage what access your child has on devices or simply turn off the Wi-Fi. Another option is to have two networks, one for the parents and one for the children, then you can just turn off the children's network or change the password on it as needed. Always give your child a warning before screens are to go off. And be aware of 'Techno tantrums'. This is when your child becomes overstimulated from watching a screen and finds it hard to calm down when they get off them. Experts talk about children needing 'green time after screen time'. This means getting them outside and moving around to help with overstimulation. And remember to always keep devices off their physical bodies. This means talking using the speaker option on mobile phones and not sitting devices on your lap to play or watch.

We live in a digital world and you cannot prevent your child from interacting with technology, but you can certainly help them to do it safely. Children have a thinner skull than we do, so if there is radiation it can get to their brain a lot easier. Some studies have shown that the energy that is transmitted from wireless devices could cause cancer and that mobile phones could increase the risk of brain tumours. The research is still ongoing but it's better to be safe than sorry I say! Remember that back in the day, no one knew that smoking caused lung cancer, or the sun caused skin cancers. Who knows what the health findings from this generation will be? I'm not taking the chance. In young children, too much screen time is also associated with such 'lovely' things as: obesity, aggressive behaviour, attention disorders and sleep problems. It can affect their brain development and speech skills. Even though you might see screen time as a bit of fun for your child, make sure you weigh up the negatives.

Chapter 10
Word Smart

PREPPING FOR SCHOOL SUCCESS

Don't stress about making sure your child can read and write before they start school. Literacy skills take a long time to master and are built up over many years. There are a lot of pre-literacy activities you can do to prepare your child to be good at reading, writing, speaking and listening. You don't need to teach them everything they will be learning at school before they even get to school. It's okay to leave some of the teaching to the teachers. Every day, many times a day, your child will encounter language in some form or another. Don't worry, you don't need a teaching degree to teach them language skills.

I can't state enough how important language skills are though, they are the foundation that all the other learning is built on. If your child has low language skills, chances are they will find all areas of academic work difficult. The amount of exposure they have had to language prior to school plays a big part in how successful they will be.

There are a lot of technical words when talking about language, so I will explain a few that your child will be exposed to, as it's probably been awhile since you've heard them, if ever:

- <u>Phoneme</u>- speech sounds, the sound letter/s make, e.g. in 'day', the letters 'a y' are making the 'ay' sound

- Grapheme- spelling choices, the letter/s, the written symbol that represent a sound; they can be a single letter (graph) e.g. the 't' and 'r' in 't r ee'; two letters (digraph) e.g. the 'ck' in 'd u ck'; three letters (trigraph) e.g. the 'igh' in 'l igh t'; or four letters (quadgraph) e.g. the 'eigh' in 'eigh t'

- Syllable- part of a word that contains a vowel sound, words can be broken up into syllables; clap for each syllable in a word or put your hand under your chin and each time your jaw drops that's one syllable, e.g. 'September' has three syllables 'Sep' 'tem' 'ber'

- Vowel- the letters 'a, e, i, o, u' and sometimes 'y' as it can sound like other vowels; a vowel sound is made by allowing a breath to flow out the mouth, without closing any part of the mouth or throat

- Consonant- all the other letters of the alphabet (excluding the vowels 'a, e, i, o, u'); a consonant sound is made by blocking air from flowing out of the mouth using the teeth, tongue, lips or palate

- CVC word- short for 'consonant-vowel-consonant' word, e.g. cat is a CVC word, milk is a CVCC word

- <u>Short vowel sound</u>- the short sound 'a, e, i, o, u' make in the words like hat, pet, fin, hop, cut

- <u>Long vowel sound</u>- the long sound 'a, e, i, o, u' make in words like hate, Pete, fine, hope cute; this saying may help… 'silent 'e' makes the vowel say its name', notice the words above all end with the silent 'e' and make all the vowels in the word say their letter name? No? Oh well, I tried…

- <u>Hard c/g sound</u>- when 'c' or 'g' meet 'a, o, u' the sound is hard, e.g. cat, cup, go, gap

- <u>Soft c/g sound</u>- when 'c' or 'g' meet 'e, i, y' the sound is soft, e.g. cent, ice, giant, gym

- <u>Blend/s</u>- joining sounds together to read a word, e.g. saying 'th i s' then 'this'; or letters put together to make a new sound, e.g. bl, dr, sp

Listening

I will talk about listening skills first as this is the skill children use from the day they are born. They listen to the world around them and they learn so much from just listening to us. You may feel silly but talk to your child about anything and everything from the day they are born. Everything is new to them and they only learn about things by listening to you. Talk about the number of things you can see, what colour things are, what position they're in, how they feel, taste, and use lots of describing words. They recognise your voice and love hearing it. Even though you may get sick of the sound of your own voice, they won't. Well not while they're still young enough to tell you otherwise. When your child gets a bit older, it's good to get into the habit of only saying things once, this way your child learns that they need to listen the first time. For this to be effective you need to look at your child, wait until they are looking at you, keep what you are saying clear, simple and short, get them to repeat what you said, wait for them to do it, then praise them for doing it. Otherwise you end up repeating yourself numerous times and they come to realise they don't need to listen to you the first time as you will end up saying it many times for them anyway.

Teach them whole body listening or 'The 5 L's', which are 'Looking eyes, Listening ears, Locked lips, Locked legs, Lap hands'. This is great for when they get to school and have to sit and listen on the carpet, they will know that they need to be looking at the speaker, listening, not speaking or making any noises, crossing their legs and putting both hands in their lap so they're not touching anything or anyone. And never interrupt your child when they're speaking, give them your undivided attention because if you want them to listen to you, you must show them the same respect. Children return the respect that they receive, or lack of.

PREPPING FOR SCHOOL SUCCESS

When they get to school they will be assessed on their ability to listen. In the meantime, here are some activities you can do with your child to help their listening skills:

- Give them verbal directions (start with 1-step, 2-step, then 3-step instructions; they need to listen to, remember and follow instructions)

- Get them to repeat verbal instructions back to you

- Play listening games (e.g. Simon Says, Hokey Pokey, Statues, Freeze, Go Fish)

- Sing songs and nursery rhymes (just you singing to them initially, singing together, then get them to sing by themselves from memory)

- Rhyming words (say rhyming words, e.g. 'at', take turns to say an 'at' rhyming word, throw in some words that don't rhyme with 'at' to see if they notice and correct you, this is called a 'non-example' and is a great way to check understanding, if they can explain why it is not right)

- Read or tell them stories (they can be listening for certain words while you read, answering questions about the story at the end, retelling the story in their own words)

- YouTube 'Jolly Phonics Phase Two' (goes through all the letter sounds with songs and actions)

- Pretend to play schools and practise the 'The 5 L's'

- Practise two-way conversations (emphasise turn taking, not interrupting, being attentive; get them to tell you three things you just talked about, then switch speaking and listening roles)

- Play memory games like 'I went shopping' (Take turns saying, *'I went shopping and bought a…'*, repeat what the person before you bought and add your own item, keep taking turns, repeating everything that has been bought and adding one more item each time. There are many variations to this game, such as *'I went to the zoo and saw a…'*, etc.)

- Questioning (ask them questions about something they just heard to check if they were listening, and not just yes/no questions either, add in wrong information to your questions to really see if they were listening, e.g. after watching a show on bats you could comment *'I didn't know bats were able to tap dance, did you?'*, encourage them to ask and answer questions)

- Odd one out (say a few words that begin with the same sound but throw in one that doesn't, e.g. car, cabbage, house, cat, they need to say the odd one out; can also be done with groups of objects, e.g. shirt, dress, phone, shorts, listen for the odd one out in the group)

Speaking

When your child says their first words it's such an exciting time. Whether it's *'Mumma'*, *'Dadda'*, *'Bubba'* or whatever it may be. And then they grow up and if you've got a child like mine you wonder some days why you encouraged them to talk so much, because now they won't stop! But no matter what kind of personality they have, they all need to learn good speaking skills, as even the shyest child will still need to speak to other children, adults and even the whole class. The more practise they've had speaking to different people in different contexts will make this a lot easier. By the time your child gets to school they should be easy to understand by unfamiliar people, speaking in sentences five to six words long, asking questions and able to retell events. Just involving them in your daily conversations helps their language skills, vocabulary and confidence immensely. Your child needs to be exposed, numerous times, to various rhymes, poems, chants and songs, where they can listen to, respond to and eventually join in with you. Using music and actions as well makes them more entertaining and memorable. Encourage lots of play-based experiences that involve the imaginative use of spoken language.

I spoke about my daughter before, she's a real have-a-chat, but I have since learned this really depends on the context. She will happily talk all day long if she's at home with her family, so when she went to school I thought she'd be great at doing oral presentations. Then when I saw a video of her first show-and-tell I was shocked. There stood my bubbly, chatty, outgoing little girl in front of her class and I could hardly hear a word she said! She spoke so softly that I was sure there was something wrong with the volume on the iPad. Then I saw her, I saw it in her face and her body language, she looked so small up there all alone, she was nervous and out of her comfort zone. My heart broke for her, she had been so excited to tell all her friends about her family, had rehearsed it many times and even had little funny stories to go with each person. But this all disappeared when she got up in front of everyone. Then it hit me, this is not a natural thing to do, to have 24 of your peers staring at you and your teacher recording you. And some children never lose that 'deer in the headlights' look when they do public speaking, and neither do some adults for that matter.

Your child will most likely be assessed on their speaking skills through oral presentations. These will be on basic topics initially, like sharing a personal experience or interest, where they get to use visual cues (e.g. poster, items) to stay on topic.

Some children will enjoy it, but most, as I've seen many times as a teacher, will find it utterly terrifying. You can work on their interaction skills to help them communicate clearly, including their articulation, body language, gestures, eye contact, and using different voice levels/volume appropriate to a situation. When they get to school these voice levels may be referred to as using their 'inside voice' (quiet) and 'outside voice' (loud).

So here it is, things you can do with your child to help them with their speaking:

- Teach them 'The 3 P's' - Prepare, Posture, Projection (Prepare- practise; Posture- stand up tall, look at the audience, make eye contact; Projection- speak slowly, clearly, loud enough to be heard by everyone)

- Talk on the phone- encourage your child to talk to friends and relatives on the phone

- Oh hello- learn how to say *'Hello'* in many different languages, and practise often; once they've mastered hello, try other words like 'goodbye, thank you, yes and no'

- Play 'The name game'- take turns naming items that belong to a certain group to see how many you can think of, e.g. colours, animals, fruits, toys

- Picture cues- after reading a story a few times, get your child to tell you the story in their own words from looking at the pictures

- Alphabet- say the letters of the alphabet and the most common sound/s each makes, until you can say the letters and your child says the sound/s. I say 'sound/s' as it's good to teach them the short and long vowel sounds, and the hard and soft c and g sounds

- Rhyming- recognising and making rhyming words when listening to rhyming stories or rhymes

- Mouth almighty- model how your mouth and tongue move to say different sounds for your child to copy, over-emphasise your mouth movements so they can see if your mouth is open/closed, where your tongue is, etc. when making a sound, they can look at their mouth in a mirror to help them copy yours

- Manners- encourage your child to always say hello, goodbye, please and thank you to people; teach them how to invite others to play and how to ask others if they can join in; model nice comments they can say to people about their appearance, food, etc.

- Likes and dislikes- talk about things you like and dislike, and why, e.g. books, shows, foods, etc.

- Talk about your day- say three things you enjoyed about your day, any you didn't or just three things you did in your day; this is nice for each family member to do every day

- Questioning- encourage your child to ask questions when they don't understand or want to know more about things; also get them to answer questions with more than one or two words

Your child will need to practise taking turns when speaking and listening. This is a good time to emphasise not talking while someone else is talking (i.e. interrupting, butting in) but being patient and waiting for your turn to speak. It's more than that though, you don't want your child just waiting for their turn to speak, not paying attention/ignoring what the other person is saying. You want them to be attentive. Of course, children always have 'super important' things to tell you, so a good habit to get into is 'Hand on hand waiting'. Hand on hand waiting means that your child sees you are busy with someone else and simply puts their hand on yours to show you that they need to tell you something. You then put your hand on their hand and this tells them (without words) that you know they want to tell you something and they can as soon as you are finished. It's a lot better than having them butt in, talk over people, tug at your clothes, tap you lots of times or do other negative things to get your attention. It also shows your child that you are interested in what they have to say, you want to hear them, but they just need to wait for their turn.

Make sure they know that it is also okay to call out if it's an emergency. Like if they or someone else is really hurt and needs an adult straight away they don't need to do 'hand on hand waiting' but make sure they understand what an emergency is. Explain to them that an emergency is things like bleeding, getting stuck somewhere, etc. and what it is not, like they want another biscuit, they saw a pretty leaf, etc.

We live in a multicultural society so it's important to explain to your child that their language is just one of many languages spoken, and that different languages may be spoken by different families and classmates. This could avoid the awkward response of, *'They talk funny'*, when your child hears someone speaking a different language. If this does happen though, just gently correct them with, *'No, they're speaking another language, they're speaking …'* This is a lot easier for them to understand if you've already discussed this with them and you've been practising speaking some basic words in other languages.

Reading

Now your child can listen to words, they can speak words, they must now be able to read words. Ha! If only it was that easy. All is not lost though, if you've been speaking to your child, reading to them, singing with them, showing them words in books and on signs, etc. they are already well on their way to learning how to read. At school children learn the connection between letters and sounds, and this will come a lot easier to them if you have done all the pre-work with them. This means exposing them to rhymes, songs, games and stories as the rhyme and rhythm help them to hear the sounds and syllables in words, which helps them learn to read. The transition is from hearing sounds, to saying sounds, to matching these sounds to written symbols (letters). Learning to read takes time, it's a process, and the following information is simply for you to use with your child when your child is ready. Don't try to implement them all at once or expect your child to be able to do them all straight away.

Above all things make reading fun and enjoyable! You want to instil a love of reading in your child. If your child enjoys reading they are far more likely to succeed at it. And don't forget that both parents need to model good reading habits. Whether you are reading to them, with them or to yourself where they can see you, show them that reading is important. When you are reading explain to them what it is and why you're reading it, e.g. this is a recipe, I'm reading it so I know what ingredients to use and how to make it. Explain new vocabulary in books but ask them what they think the word means first before telling them. Don't worry about reading children's books with words that may seem too 'hard' for them, reading these words aloud and discussing them will develop your child's vocabulary. Even when your child is old enough to read independently, still read aloud to them, it allows them to hear more difficult vocabulary and still enjoy the act of being read to.

Encourage your child to pretend to read and make up stories to go with the illustrations in books. This gives them the early confidence they need to see themselves as successful 'readers'. When reading aloud to your child use different voices for different characters to make it more interesting. Make sure you can both see the book and read at a pace appropriate to their age and interest level. When reading with your child, relate topics in the book back to your child's own experiences to make it more meaningful. This way they can connect with the text, either at a personal level as something from their life, something they've seen in others' lives or something they've seen in another text.

The more books you read with your child, the more comfortable they will be with books. And if your child is like most children, they will come to have favourites that they want to read many times, many more times than you want to. This is a good thing though. It may not seem like it as you're reading *One Mole Digging a Hole* for the twentieth time, but children learn through repetition. Read them stories with repeated patterns in them so they can join in and predict what comes next. This allows them to engage with the story, and as they become more familiar with stories, you can pause to let them say the next part.

There are many pre-reading activities you can be doing with your child to prepare them to be a reader. Here are some to focus on:

- Concepts of print- how to hold a book, turn the pages one at a time, read from front to back, finger pointing to the words to show that we read from left to right and top to bottom with a return sweep to the left; talk about the features of a book (front and back cover, author, illustrator, spine, title page, blurb); difference between pictures, letters, words, sentences; punctuation meanings (capital letter, full stop, comma, question mark, exclamation mark, quotation/speech marks, spaces between words)

- Environmental print- pointing out signs, labels, etc. when out, e.g. *'That sign says Stop'*; having their name on numerous things so they can recognise it, e.g. on their door

- Sound awareness- finding other words that start with the same sound, e.g. *'Claire starts with the same sound as cat, coat*'; sing songs together and clap rhythmically along with them; use flashcards with letters on them and say the sounds for each

- Letter awareness- saying the alphabet; identifying letters in words (especially in their own name); identify letters in upper and lower case (say the letter name, sound, a word beginning with that letter); knowing that words are made up of letters; name objects that begin with the same letter; point to words in a text that begin with the same letter; using hands-on activities to memorise letters, e.g. making letters with playdough, making your body into a letter, drawing the letter with your finger on your child's back

- Rhyme awareness- finding rhyming words in books; teaching them 'word families' (e.g. 'at' rat, cat, bat, etc.)

When your child is showing these behaviours and abilities, they may be ready to learn to read. If not, do activities like these with them. When doing the 'concepts of print' activities, explain to them that the author's name is written first and they write the story. And the illustrator's name is written next and they draw or paint the pictures. Sometimes there is only one name, and this means the person is the author and the illustrator. The 'blurb', children love saying this word, is the writing on the back cover that tells us about the story. A little note on letter and sound awareness, letters don't have to be taught in alphabetical order. It's better to teach them the letters 's, a, t, p, i, n' first so they can start to read a few simple words right away. Plus, the letters in their name of course. When they realise they can read some words it's very exciting for them and keeps them motivated to learn more. To learn each letter, your child needs to be able to identify the letter visually and memorise the name of the letter and the sound the letter makes. Then, just for fun, there are letters that make more than one sound, and the fact that each letter can be written two ways, upper and lower case, and even in different fonts!

Your child will need a lot of exposure to letters before they can memorise them all. It takes time and repetition. When teaching your child 'word families' you are helping them to see patterns in reading. This allows them to begin reading by grouping sets of letters within a word. To get technical, the first part of a word is called the 'onset' and the last part of the word is called the 'rime'. Word families have a similar 'rime', but the 'onset' changes, e.g. 'at' in bat, cat, hat. Learning word families means that if they can recognise one word like 'cat', then they can read many 'at' words as they have the same rime with only the onset changing. Some good word families to start with are the two letter ones like, 'an, at, ap, it, in, ip.'

WORD SMART

1000 books before school

The United States has a great program called '*1000 Books Before School*'. It encourages parents to read 1,000 books to their child before they get to school, and while this sounds like a lot, if you break it down, it's very manageable. If you start reading to your child from birth, you need to read 200 books each year to reach 1,000 books by the time they are five. And in fact, if you read just one book to your child each day, by the time they are five they will have read 1,825 books! And it doesn't have to be all different books either! It's just the number of times they need to be read to before they become readers themselves. If you read to your child for just 10 minutes each day you expose them to more than 600,000 words in one year! Every day counts! Every book counts!

There are many great children's picture books out there. But if you're unsure where to start, these are some wonderful authors to look out for: Pamela Allen, Jeannie Baker, Aaron Blabey, Nick Bland, Rod Campbell, Eric Carle, Julia Donaldson, Dr Seuss, Mem Fox, Jackie French, Eric Hill, Pat Hutchins, Stephen Michael King, Alison Lester, Margaret Wild, just to name a few... You can also check out 'The Premier's Reading Challenge' website, that has a great booklist each year for Early Childhood (ages 0-5), https://readingchallenge.education.qld.gov.au/about/booklists.

Print rich environment

It's important to provide a 'Print-rich environment' for your child where they are regularly exposed to words on posters, charts, books, labels, signs, etc. Point out letters and words as you see them and in time your child will be doing the same. Just keep it fun! Play simple word games that encourage them to listen, identify and manipulate the sounds in words. Just focus on the first letter in words initially by asking them, *'What is that letter?'*, *'What sound does that letter make?'* or *'What other words start with that sound?'* Play games like 'I spy' but say, *'I spy with my little eye, something that begins with the s sound.'*

Go to the library regularly with your child, they may have an early years program with free activities and storytelling. I know my local libraries have a program for young children that is free to join and gives you a free library bag, picture book, DVD, reading strategies, nursery rhymes and songs book. Books can be expensive, so this is a great way to expose your child to numerous books by borrowing library books for free. You can also buy cheap books from charity stores, markets or request them as birthday presents. I always like to give a book to my children as part of their birthday, Easter and Christmas presents. And read them books relevant to events happening in their lives e.g. books on birthdays, starting school, going on a plane, becoming a big brother/sister, Easter, Christmas, etc.

Comprehension

To help your child's comprehension skills get into the habit of asking them questions before, during and after reading. Show your child the front cover of the book and ask them what they think the story is going to be about, this is 'predicting'. While reading, ask them what they think is going to happen next, this is 'inferring'. Ask your child if they have ever done something like the character in the story, this is 'connecting'. At the end of the book get them to tell you what happened in their own words, this is 'summarising'. Discuss what they liked and didn't like about the story. Model your own opinions about a text. Expose them to different types of texts, imaginative (fiction, pretend) and informative (non-fiction, real). Try reading them a story and not showing them the pictures, then getting them to draw what they think a character from the story looks like, this is 'visualising'. It's easy to ask your child 'literal' questions, such as, what they did, where they went or who was in a story. Your child answers these questions by simply recalling information. Also ask them 'inferential' questions. Such as, why they thought something happened, how the story could have ended differently. These questions make them think.

Sounding out

Once your child can identify single sounds the next step is being able to blend these sounds together to read words, also called 'sounding out'. Try using a two or three letter word, e.g. sat, point to the letters and say each sound 's a t'. Then start back at the beginning of the word. Slide your finger slowly under the letters as you stretch the sounds and put them together. Use words where each letter makes its 'normal' sound, like those CVC (consonant, vowel, consonant) words I talked about, e.g. pin, tap, sit, etc. They can then use this skill when they begin reading and come across a word they don't know. Never jump in and tell them the word, give them a chance to work it out by themselves and if they can't, prompt them to 'sound it out'.

Make sure your child knows that you're proud of their reading efforts e.g. *'Great sounding out'* or *'You tried really hard to sound out that tricky word.'* This builds their confidence to keep trying. If your child still has difficulty sounding out the word, say the sounds with them, e.g. *'Let's sound it out together, c a t, cat.'* If your child is having to 'sound out' every word on every page, the book is too hard for them at this stage. Even children who can decode words and read fluently still might not be able to comprehend what they are reading. If they can't understand what they are reading, there is really no point to reading it. Reading then becomes a chore, it's hard work sounding out every word. When your child has worked through a difficult word or sentence, encourage them to reread it. This will give them more practise with the words and allow them to focus on the meaning of the sentence.

Sight words

As if learning to read wasn't hard enough, there are words in the English language that defy all logic. There is no way your child can 'sound them out' as they don't sound anything like the letters used to make the word. Words like 'the', 'was' and 'one' for example, are what we call 'sight words', as the only way to learn them is by memorising them by sight. Think, *'See the word, say the word.'* And unfortunately, a lot of the most common, or high frequency words used in stories are 'sight words'. There are a few popular lists of sight words, like the Dolch and Fry lists you can practise with your child. These can be accessed on my website. But don't get overwhelmed when looking at these lists as they have literally hundreds of words! Just start working on a few sight words at a time and practise them regularly, when your child is ready. This builds up their sight word vocabulary, their reading confidence and is essential for them to become fluent readers.

When you come across a 'sight word' talk about how it's different, e.g. *'That's a tricky word, that's one of those sight words. The 'ai' in that word makes the sound 'e'* (short e sound). *So, the word is s ai d, said.'* Display sight words at home, practise them in the car, at the table when eating, whatever and whenever is best for your family. Above all else, make learning sight words fun! Check out www.sightwords.com for some excellent free, printable resources to use with your child. Some ideas to learn sight words include:

- Using flash cards

- Looking for sight words in books

- Games- Sight Words Bingo, Go Fish, Memory

- Making the words- using playdough, toothpicks, small stones, etc.

- Writing the words- rainbow letters (different colour for each letter), in sand with fingers or sticks, on cement with chalk, whiteboard markers on whiteboard, paint them, etc.

- Fly swat- put sight words on print outs of flies, use a fly swatter to swat the correct sight word given, builds speed in recognising sight words (please buy a clean fly swat to use just for this activity, don't drag out the one covered in fly bits, gross!)

- Out & About app- free, first 100 sight words, in visual and spoken form, games, activity ideas

Home readers

Once your child starts getting 'home readers' from school, it's important that someone listens to them read these books every day. Yes, life will get in the way, cooking dinner, having breakfast, looking after other children, but it only takes 10 minutes a day of reading to help your child be a successful reader. These initial home readers will be very basic, short and are usually referred to as 'decodable' or 'predictable' texts. They are mostly books where each sentence in the book is the same except for one word that will change on each page, which can be worked out (inferred), with the help of a picture. For example, 'I can run' (picture of a child running), 'I can swim' (picture of a child swimming)' etc. As they read these books multiple times their fluency improves, and they are proud to be reading. They will read them aloud, tracking each word with their finger underneath, reading at a steady pace and attempting to work out unknown words.

They will learn lots of reading strategies at school to help them become better readers, some may even have cute animal names like these to help remember them:

- Eagle Eye- look at the pictures to help you figure out the words

- Lips the Fish- get your lips ready to say the first few sounds of a word

- Stretchy Snake- stretch the sounds out in a word to figure out the word

- Skippy Frog- skip the word and read on to the end of the sentence, then hop back and try again

- Chunky Monkey- look for a smaller chunk you know inside a word

- Tryin' Lion- look back over a word or sentence, try another strategy

- Dot the Giraffe- look at the punctuation, read with expression

- Flippy the Dolphin- if the short vowel sound doesn't make sense, try the long vowel sound

- Helpful Kangaroo- if you've tried all the other strategies and still don't know, ask for help

Lastly on reading...

Be patient. The single most important thing you can do is to make reading an enjoyable experience with lots of encouragement and praise at their early attempts. Every child learns at their own pace, it is not a race! Never compare your child's reading to another child's. It doesn't matter what reading level the other children are on, focus on your child and help them to succeed. And if you are reading regularly, doing different pre-reading activities with them, you'll instil an early love of reading and give them the best chance at reading success.

Writing

Before you know it those scribbles your child is doing turn into letters, words and sentences. When your child starts to show that they are ready to write letters, it's good to begin with letters in their name and the letters 's, a, t, p, i, n'. They can then write small words (e.g. I, a, at, it, in, sit, sat, etc.). They will more than likely move on to writing names of familiar people (e.g. Mum, Dad, Mia) and high-frequency words (e.g. and, the, can, etc.). When your child is in the early stages of writing, they will rely a lot on being able to sound out words and write the letters they think are making the sounds, known as 'phonetic spelling'. This may begin as just a 'c' to represent the word 'can' or words like 'luv' for 'love and 'kat' for cat. You can talk about punctuation with them as they start to recognise that capital letters are used for names and to start sentences, full stops are at the end of most sentences, and there are spaces between words.

This space between words is often referred to as a 'finger space', meaning they put their fingertip down on the paper at the end of a word before they write the next word, this makes sure a space is left between the words. Make sure when they are writing their name they are doing it in the correct case, with upper case letter for the first letter and lower case for the remaining letters. Please don't teach them how to write in all upper case as this just needs to be corrected. Keep an eye out for letter reversals, where your child might be writing a 'b' for 'd' or '9' for 'P' and correct as needed. They are very common with early writers. Your child might ask you to write words for them, always encourage them to have a go first, even if it's just scribble and then even if you do write letters or words for them, get them to trace over yours or copy it underneath.

All attempts at writing should be encouraged, with their effort being the focus of your praise. They may do some scribbles as part of their play as a message, e.g. a menu, shopping list, etc. Ask them to 'read' their initial attempts at 'writing' to you. Always encourage them to have-a-go at writing their name on anything they make. Practise writing and spelling using word families (e.g. an, man, can, fan) and CVC words (e.g. dog, rat, bin, etc.). Model good writing habits for your child, let them see you writing a shopping list, a job list, etc. Teach them correct posture and pencil grip for writing, how to construct each letter (e.g. where to start, which direction to go, where to end). Remember to always start writing a letter at the top, not the bottom. Check out my website for some letter writing templates.

Just like reading, writing takes a lot of practise and the more fun you make it, the more your child will be interested in doing it. Some writing activities include:

- Tracing over repeated lines (zigzag, curved, straight, etc.) that go from left to right

- Write with chalk or water on a paintbrush on the footpath

- Make letters and words with playdough, small blocks

- Use your finger to write in the steam of the bathroom, with finger paints, in shaving cream

- Use a stick or your finger to write in sand, dirt, etc.

- Provide your child with lots of writing materials to get creative with (e.g. different coloured paper, cardboard, envelopes, pens, pencils, crayons)

- Set up a 'writing station' in your house with a small desk and chair and writing materials

- Write letters to people (e.g. a friend, family member, Easter Bunny, Santa Claus, etc.)

- Trace between the lines of bubble writing letters, staying inside the lines

- Use dot-to-dot to make letters, following through each dot

- Practise writing different sized letters, big/small, and on smaller pieces of paper (children tend to write very large initially)

- Use a keyboard to practise typing lower- and upper-case letters

Chapter 11
Number Smart

○ △ ▢ ▭

0 1 2 3 4 5 6 7 8 9 10

Literacy and numeracy go hand in hand and will be the main academic areas of learning when your child gets to school. They will probably be referred to as English and Maths/Mathematics at school. And just like literacy you have been building up your child's numeracy skills ever since they were a baby. You have helped them develop numeracy and maths skills through everyday activities like counting, singing number songs, looking at shapes, and talking about sizes. Numeracy skills are best learnt through play so make these everyday numeracy activities and experiences fun and relaxed. Numeracy includes concepts such as numbers, patterns, measuring, shapes, time, days, location and answering questions.

Numeracy activities

Some things you might already be doing or could start doing with your child to build their numeracy skills include:

- Reading stories with numeracy concepts (e.g. *'The Very Hungry Caterpillar'* by Eric Carle; *'One Fish, Two Fish, Red Fish, Blue Fish'* by Dr Seuss; *'Ten Little Fingers and Ten Little Toes'* by Mem Fox)

- Counting anything and everything (e.g. shells at the beach, fruit at the shop, toys, fingers, toes, steps you take when walking, stairs, cutlery as they set the table)

- Singing number songs and rhymes (e.g. *'Five little ducks'*, *'One, two, three, four, five'*, using actions)

- Speed up or slow down (play or sing music/songs at different speeds, dance, jump or play instruments slow or fast)

- Number hunt (go for a walk and look for numbers e.g. letterboxes, houses, number plates, road signs; at home e.g. clocks, phones, books, remote controls; at the shops e.g. prices, quantities)

- Use a growth chart to record your child's height

- Cooking together (they can help to stir, pour, mix, etc. helps concepts of counting, measuring, adding and estimating)

- Play board games, card games and puzzles with numbers and shapes (e.g. snap, dominoes, pairs, Uno, snakes and ladders)

- Play outside games (e.g. hopscotch, skittles and *'What's the time Mr Wolf?'*)

- Race for a place (e.g. race each other, toy cars, etc. for 1st, 2nd, 3rd)

- Use a device to draw shapes, type numbers, etc. or find fun numeracy apps and websites (e.g. www.mathsisfun.com, YouTube *'Numberjacks'* for fun number stories)

- Make numbers, shapes, etc. with playdough and other materials

- Estimate before counting (e.g. fruit or vegetables at the shop, popcorn, toys)

- Nature walk (collect leaves, sticks, pebbles, etc. and sort them into groups based on size, colour, shape)

- Order toys, etc. from shortest to tallest

- Sharing is caring (share out food, etc. into equal shares; cutting food into halves, quarters)

- Money bags (sort coins into groups based on colour, size, value; hand over and collect money at the shops)

- Water or sand play (fill up and empty lots of different sized containers)

- Use a calendar to count down to important events by crossing off days

- It's about time (e.g. Playschool's *'Rocket clock'*, clocks in the home, using a timer to time things you do)

- Shape hunt (e.g. find three cubes inside/outside the house, four squares in a magazine)

- Location, location, location (put toys in different positions and discuss where they are, e.g. under the chair; do a mini obstacle course e.g. go over the ball, through the tunnel; make a treasure map to follow; collect maps from zoos or parks and use them)

- Make a chart where your child can put a sticker on each time it rains or each time it is sunny

Mathematical language

Your child will learn a lot of their numeracy skills from listening to you as well as doing things for themselves. Try changing your tone of voice to describe concepts e.g. a big voice to describe something big, or a little voice to describe something little. Just make it fun. Here are some ways you can incorporate mathematical language into your day:

- At home (e.g. *'This cup has more and this one has less'*, *'Where's the matching shoe to this one?'*)

- Out and about (e.g. *'The lift is going up'*, *'That's a tall man'*, *'That tree is near the lake'*)

- Food (e.g. *'Let's put half the popcorn in this bowl and half in the other bowl'*, *'Let's have two pieces of toast'*, *'How many plates do we need?'*, *'Let's share these grapes, one for you, one for me'*)

- Time (e.g. *'7 o'clock, it's time for bed'*, *'We will have lunch at 12 o'clock'*, *'The movie starts in 1 hour'*)

- Shapes and patterns (e.g. *'Let's look for all the squares'*, *'What's the pattern with the beads?'*)

- Sizes (e.g. compare the different sizes of things 'big, small, long, short, heavy, light')

- Groups (after grouping items talk about how they are the same/different)

- Location (use words to describe where things are 'over, under, on top of')

It can be tricky

It's important to always encourage your child's attempts at numeracy. If they get something wrong, ask them how they got their answer, get them to explain their thinking, their reasoning. This is a very important skill to master. Sometimes doing it this way allows your child to discover their own errors and fix them. Other times you will need to correct them and explain why that's the actual answer. Allow your child time to think, just wait and listen to them, don't feel the need to jump in with the correct answer. Some children need that extra processing time, especially if the concept is new to them. Watch out for number reversals when your child is writing numbers and correct as needed. Children often reverse the numbers 2, 5, 6 and 9, but I've also seen 3, 4 and 7 reversed, so it's pretty much 1 and 8 that are safe. This is usually just developmental and can be corrected with lots of practise, best done with fun activities such as writing numbers in sand, steam, chalk, paint, etc.

Mathematical concepts

When your child gets to school, Mathematics will be broken down into: Number and Algebra; Measurement and Geometry; Statistics and Probability. All big names for basic concepts in the early years. I will explain each of these in more detail next. In all three mathematical concepts however, your child will need to demonstrate the skills of understanding, fluency, problem-solving and reasoning to be successful. By understanding I mean being able to connect ideas like number names, numerals and quantities to one another. Fluency includes accurately counting numbers in sequences, comparing objects and continuing patterns.

Problem solving is being able to use materials to model real problems, sorting objects, using known concepts to solve new problems and discussing answers. And reasoning includes explaining comparisons of measurements, creating patterns and explaining their thinking.

Number and Algebra

Number is self-explanatory but algebra, really? For young children? How could they possibly understand algebra? Well it's obviously not high school algebra, but the concepts of patterns and sorting that form their initial understanding of algebra. I will break down some of the mathematical concepts under the heading of 'Number and Algebra' that they will need to understand in their first years of school:

- Place value- the value of a numeral, e.g. 6 is 6 ones, 12 is 1 ten and 2 ones, 25 is 2 tens and 5 ones

- Counting- by rote; naming numbers in sequences, to and from 10, then to and from 20; counting from any given number (not always counting up from 1 and down from 20); counting objects only once; pointing to objects to count them; understanding different arrangements of the same number of objects doesn't affect how many there are (called 'rational count'); last number counted answers the 'how many' question

- Identifying numbers- connecting numbers in numerals, words, pictures, quantities; including zero

- Subitising- means being able to instantly recognise the number of objects or dots in a small group without the need to count them

- Ordering and comparing- small collections of objects using words like 'more, less, same as, not the same as'

- Ordinal numbers- 'first, second, third', up to 'tenth' to show position

- Addition and sharing- using small groups of numbers and real-life examples, hands-on/concrete materials, pictures; counts total of two groups of objects up to a sum of ten

- Money- recognise coins and notes

- Sort and classify- with objects by size, colour, shape, use

- Patterns- copy, continue, create and describe patterns (with objects, drawings, sounds, movements); recognising patterns in the world around us (e.g.

tiles, flowers); AB patterns like red, yellow, red, yellow (repeating patterns of shapes, numbers, letters, beads, anything really)

Measurement and Geometry

Geometry is basically looking at sizes, shapes and positions in the early years. It's these early concepts that build the foundations for more difficult geometrical concepts later at school. I will break down some of the topics that come under the heading of 'Measurement and Geometry' that your child will need to understand in their first years at school:

- Direct and indirect comparisons- 'direct' meaning to place one object against another and measure; 'indirect' meaning to measure objects using another object; to decide which is longer, heavier or holds more, and explain why

- Using language to compare- tall/taller, heavy/heavier, holds more/less, longer/shorter, same/different

- Sort objects- according to length (how long it is), mass (how heavy it is), capacity (how much it holds)

- Heft- balance an item in each hand to work out which is heavier/lighter

- Measuring instruments- scales for weight, ruler/tape measure for length, containers/jugs for volume

- Compare and order duration of events- events that occur on certain days, sequencing events in time order (e.g. before, during, after)

- Time- day/night, days of the week, months of the year; time to the hour; concept of seconds, minutes, hours

- Sort, describe and name two-dimensional (2D) shapes and three-dimensional (3D) objects- square, circle, triangle, rectangle, sphere, cube, cone, cylinder, rectangular prism; features of each; shapes in the environment

- Describe position and movement- also known as location and direction; using language like 'between, near, next to, forward, toward, under, over'; following and giving simple directions

Statistics and Probability

In the early years 'statistics' is simply answering yes/no questions to collect information. And 'probability' is looking at the language used to say how likely something is to happen, e.g. observations about the weather, events. Some concepts covered in 'Statistics and Probability' include:

- Data- information collected by counting or measuring items, e.g. picture graphs

- Interpreting data- making sense of information collected, explaining results gathered, sorting information into similarities and differences

- Making inferences- using what you know to make a guess about something you don't know

- Language of chance/likelihood- certain, likely, even chance, unlikely, impossible, never, always

- Asking questions- about themselves, others, familiar objects, events, etc.

- Data displays- graphs used to show responses to questions or used to answer simple questions

Chapter 12
Alarm Bells

I have talked about a lot of things you can do to prepare you and your child for school, but what if, despite all your hard work, they're just not getting it? Your child may be very sensitive, strong-willed or have a diagnosed disability, all of these things will make the job of preparing them for school a bit trickier. But not impossible. You may just need to approach things in different ways to suit your child, their abilities, their strengths and their weaknesses. You need to do what works best for you, your child and your family. If you notice that your child is not developing at the same rate as their peers and it's becoming more and more noticeable, whether it be in speech, movement or behaviour, get help!

Don't stress, don't be in denial, get them checked out. If you are concerned about your child's development take them to see a specialist, your doctor (GP), a paediatrician, a Speech Language Pathologist (SLP), an Occupational Therapist (OT), whoever you think is best suited to the issues your child is having. If it turns out to be nothing, good, you can stress a little less now. Or you can always get a second opinion if you're not convinced. You, as the parent, know your child better than anyone. Trust your gut. Or then again if a lot of specialists are telling you the same thing, maybe you need to start listening...

Some concerns won't come up until your child is at school as they may be more noticeable compared to their peers. Like auditory processing problems, where your child can't easily turn the words that they're hearing into mental pictures that make sense as quickly as the teacher is talking. It can be hard to hear or accept that your child is a bit 'different'. But once you stop trying to change your child, and change your expectations instead, life will be a lot easier for you, your child, everyone. Depending on their diagnosis, you may need to miss out on some things if you know they will upset your child. But you need to ask yourself, *'Is it really worth the drama?'* You may need to make a lot of compromises, but again think to yourself, *'Is the tantrum and melt down worth it?'* Children are all wired differently. If you are ever unsure, it can be helpful to refer to a developmental checklist as a bit of a guide as to what your child should be doing at their age and what are some warning signs to look out for. I've put some developmental checklists on my website to help you with this. These are pretty general, children develop at different rates and not always according to a checklist, but they're a good guide nonetheless.

Biology can play a part in your child's development as well, as girls and boys can develop certain abilities at different rates and tend to be interested in different things. Girls tend to develop language and fine motor skills earlier than boys. It sounds very stereotypical but after teaching for so many years, in general, boys do like to run around and play rough and tumble and girls like to dress up and play with dolls. It may just be hard-wired into them or how they've been raised, but there's a noticeable difference between genders.

In the early years at school girls tend to enjoy colouring in and listening to stories whereas boys tend to enjoy outdoor play and using hands-on materials.

Separation

Separation anxiety is a normal part of development. It's the fear of being away from their care givers and it begins when your child is a baby. But by the time they go to school, for most children, it has gradually passed. If your child's separation anxiety is longer-lasting and is affecting both of your lives, you may need to get some professional help. When they are close to school age you should organise some pre-visits to your child's future school to help them adjust to their new setting and the physical environment. The more familiar they are with the setting, the people, the routines, the less anxious about going there they should be. They will come to know it as a safe place, just like home. Outside of visiting the school you could leave them with another trusted adult for short periods to get them used to being separated from you. Always tell your child something like, *'I'm going to leave now but I will be back.'* This prepares and reassures them. Then when you do come back, reassure them again with, *'See I told you I would be back.'* You can gradually increase the time you're away from them.

Make sure these separation and reunion experiences are positive ones and don't try to avoid separations from your child as this can make the problem worse. They need practice at being separated from you to get better at it, it's about facing their fears rather than avoiding them. Never try to sneak away from your child without saying goodbye as this can make them even more upset and confused when they can't find you. As well as make it harder for them to separate from you next time. While we are talking about things to avoid, never downplay their emotions. If they are upset, acknowledge that they're upset. It can get frustrating if your child's separation issues are long-lasting and may be making you late for work, annoyed, etc. but don't stoop to calling them a cry baby, etc. It can get hard but being negative about their separation issues doesn't help anyone. Be sure to give them lots of praise when they do separate easily from you to build up their self-esteem.

There are some great picture books on separation that you can read with your child to show them that they're not alone feeling this way and can give them some other strategies to help. *'The Invisible String'* by Patrice Karst and *'The Kissing Hand'* by Audrey Penn, are lovely stories about dealing with separation you can read with your child. When they do get to school make sure they are getting to class in a good mood. You can do this by playing upbeat music in the car on the way to school, singing fun songs in the car, playing games or just being silly with them. Leave them in a happy mood, doing an activity that they enjoy. Make sure you too are in a happy mood, so they can see that you too are happy for them to be in this safe place.

You can even organise with your child's teacher to get your child doing a 'special' job for them each morning, like tidying up the bookshelf, sharpening the pencils, whatever it might be to preoccupy them and get their mind on other things. Don't linger when saying goodbye. Make it short and sweet. Just like 'Pulling off a Band-Aid' from the start of this book. Let the school know whatever you are doing with your child that helps ease their anxiety, so they too can be doing the same. It can help to let your child take an item they love from home with them, such as a small teddy or blanket, to help them feel safe, but be sure to slowly phase out bringing this. Just by having this for the morning, or even having it in their bag to see every now and then, can help them settle.

Sensory Processing Disorder (SPD) and Autism Spectrum Disorder (ASD)

If your child has a Sensory Processing Disorder (SPD) or Autism Spectrum Disorder (ASD) they tend to have different reactions to what we would class as every day experiences. Even though SPD and ASD are different disorders, I have put them together here as they have similar sensitivities. Your child may have a heightened sensitivity to sound, colour, texture, movement, light, touch, taste or people. These will need to be accounted for to make them comfortable. Children with ASD, and children in general actually, thrive on routines and can get upset when there is a change to their routine. Make sure you prepare them in advance if you know

ALARM BELLS

something different is happening. They can get fixated on one subject and take things that you say literally.

As a parent you need to be aware of your child's 'triggers', what sets them off, and try to minimise these whenever you can. It's important to make sure that your child's school and teachers are aware of these as well and tell them what works best for your child. This is not a time to pretend your child is fine and that they will not have any problems fitting in with the learning environment. If you know that's honestly not true, your school cannot help your child if you are hiding information about your child from them. Remember it's a partnership between you, the school and your child, everyone needs to be on the same page as everyone wants what is best for your child. It's not a matter of waiting to see if the school will recognise your child's needs, that wastes valuable learning time and does not help your child. Be open and honest about your child's needs and abilities. You know how they react to different situations, what calms them down, what they enjoy, share this information with their school and help everyone.

There is a good picture book called, *'Ellie Bean the Drama Queen'* by Jennie Harding, that can help children, parents and teachers better understand children with sensory processing issues. And *'All My Stripes: A Story for Children with Autism'* by Shaina Rudolph and Danielle Royer, can help your child and others understand Autism. If your child has Autism make sure you check out Sue Larkey's website www.suelarkey.com.au and her 'Tip sheets' on there. It is full of very useful tips for parents and teachers. She is one of the Autism gurus. Just one of the great things you'll find on there is a 'Student Profile Sheet' where you can list your child's strengths, challenges, meltdown triggers, behaviours before meltdowns, best way to approach them, sensory notes, and who the child works well with. The information you provide on a sheet like this would help anyone working with your child when they get to school.

It's important you seek a diagnosis for your child, as Tony Attwood (another Autism guru) states, *'Without a diagnosis children are judged, with a diagnosis they can be supported.'* And you too can be supported, with the funding and understanding that comes along with a diagnosis. If you are concerned about your child, take them to a paediatrician and get a professional opinion, even if it is just to rule out a disorder.

Speech Language Pathologist (SLP)

Your child may have recognisable speech difficulties and need to see a SLP. It may be that they have 'speech difficulties' where they have trouble with their pronunciation, a lisp or a stutter. They may have 'language difficulties' where they find it hard to express themselves through spoken language or understand what is said to them. You or other people might have difficulty understanding what your child is saying or your child knows fewer words than their peers. These can all be signs of a speech language disorder. If you, or your child's doctor, think your child may have a speech or language delay, get your child assessed by a SLP. The sooner the better. As a lot of these issues can be corrected before they get to school or in the early years of school. Don't wait until your child is at school and think that the school will fix it, or it will be free then. This isn't the case. Schools don't provide one-on-one therapy for your child with a Speech Pathologist or Occupational Therapist. This is something you need to organise privately, and best done before they get to school or as soon as it's apparent. Check with your GP as Medicare can help with access to therapists. Speech Pathology Australia has developed a 'Communication Milestone Kit' for children aged 1-5 that explains what your child should be able to understand and say at different ages. You can find it on my website.

Occupational Therapist (OT)

Maybe you're noticing your child is slow to learn everyday skills that we take for granted. Those functional skills necessary for everyday life and learning. They may need to see an OT to help them better access their environment, both at home and school. An OT could help your child to learn self-care skills for eating, toileting, dressing and personal hygiene; adaptive skills to help them be more organised, develop play skills and function in a classroom; or cognitive skills to help with their attention, problem solving and memory. They could also help with your child's sensory processing skills which they need to be able to concentrate, sit still and handle different materials in their environment. Maybe your child is having difficulty with fine and gross motor activities, all of these issues could be worked on with the help of an OT. Your child's needs, whatever they may be, could impact their ability to access the curriculum when they get to school or impact their ability to engage in the school environment. If this is the case, you need to work with your child's school to make sure their needs are being catered for.

Learning styles

We also need to be aware that children have different learning styles, so sometimes what works for one child, doesn't work for another. This can be true even with children from the same family. Some children learn best by doing, some by seeing, some by listening, and some by speaking. And just for fun, most people have a mix of learning styles they prefer, depending on what they are learning. It's important to know what your child's dominant learning style is, as this knowledge will help you to teach them and help them to understand concepts a lot easier. It's also important so you don't expect your child, who may be a physical learner, to sit still and passively listen for a long time. They are going to get distracted and restless and not be taking anything in.

Instead of talking to them, which an aural learner would enjoy, you need to get them doing things with their hands, learning by doing, e.g. don't talk to them about shapes, give them shape puzzles to do.

To get technical here is a list of some learning styles, see if you can spot your child's dominant one, and maybe your own:

- Verbal (linguistic)- using words, speaking, writing
- Aural (auditory)- using sound, music
- Visual (spatial)- seeing pictures, images
- Physical (kinaesthetic)- using body, hands, touch
- Logical (mathematical)- using logic, reasoning, systems
- Social (interpersonal)- learning in groups, with others
- Solitary (intrapersonal)- working alone, independently

Fair?

'Fair doesn't mean everyone gets the same, fair means everyone gets what they need' (Rick Riordan). I love this saying, it's so true! I used to have it up on my wall next to my desk in the classroom as a reminder. We talk a lot about 'being fair' and 'treating everyone the same' but it is not possible to treat everyone the same and be fair at the same time. Children all have different needs and you need to do different things for them to help them to succeed. Even the idea of 'success' is

different for all children and dependent on their abilities. It could be a child getting to hold a sensory toy to help them focus on the mat or a child getting to use a weighted bag on their lap to help them sit still. This is not giving them 'special attention' over the other children, it's giving them what they need to access learning. It's not about the teacher having favourites, it's about wanting all children to succeed and be able to participate in the classroom equally.

Afterword

You did it! Go you! You got through all 12 chapters, or you've just skipped to this part. Either way I just wanted to let you know that it's okay if you don't remember all the advice I've shared in this book, you can always flick back to bits as you need them. That's called life. We all have good days and bad days, just like our children. Some days you will feel like you're winning at this whole parent thing and other days you will feel like a complete failure, struggling to survive. Just don't let the bad days consume you, or rule your thoughts, focus on the good days, and yes there will be many. Be grateful for every day you have and make the most of each day. Make sure at the end of each day you give yourself some time to reflect on the day and think of at least three things that were good about that day. They can be as little or big as you like. It could simply be that you had a yummy snack, you got a nice message from someone or your child gave you a hug. It's even nicer to keep them in a 'Gratitude Journal' so you can reflect on them every now and then, especially when you've had a hard day. *'Don't wait for things to get easier, simpler, better. Life will always be complicated. Learn to be happy right now. Otherwise, you'll run out of time.'* (Author unknown)

I think as a parent we tend to say, '*We just want our child to be happy.*' But there are so many underlying things to make this happen. We also want them to be, 'Healthy, loving, included, honest, kind, responsible, respectful, to feel safe, have self-control, have good friends, and make good choices'. It just doesn't roll off the tongue as easily as, '*Happy*', and it makes us sound less like a crazy parent. Then as a parent if we're asked, '*What's your job as a parent?*', answering, '*To love them*', is a pretty easy one. But really, we need to do so much more, and we do… in reality our 'job' is to be: a good role model, be loving, consistent, reliable, make sure they have a healthy diet, adequate sleep and exercise, speak to them as we wish for them to speak to us, listen to them, catch them being good, and focus on their positive behaviours.

At the same time, we need to look after our own emotional wellbeing. We need to stay positive and try to never hold a grudge, blame others, yell, and remember to choose our battles. There's no point in arguing over everything, stick to the important stuff, the stuff that matters, that's the stuff you need to work on, not argue about. You want your child to look back on their childhood and their schooling in years to come as fun and enjoyable, some of the best times in their life. Not as something they need to try and forget when they're older. You can set your child up early to be successful at school and life in general. This may take a bit of work on your behalf, but the rewards far outweigh the effort put in. As your child becomes more independent and automatically

AFTERWORD

does all the things you've been practising over and over with them you can stand back and be amazed by this wonderful human being you've created. It may even make you a bit sad when you realise they don't need you to do things like dress them, bath them, etc. anymore. Never underestimate how important you are in your child's life, in their success. They look up to you and you need to honour that.

It is true what they say, *'The days are long, but the years are short'* (Gretchen Rubin). You only have your children for but a moment in time. Remember this, be present, enjoy them, love them and help them to succeed in life. Whether you are a parent by choice, chance or other, it is an important 'job', probably the most important you'll ever have. You are shaping the future, how amazing you are to be preparing these little people for a world you don't even know about yet. But to set them up as lifelong, successful learners, this, this will help them no matter what the future holds for them. The fact that you took time out of your own life to read this book, to benefit them, speaks volumes of you as a parent.

You want your child to succeed at school? Well I've told you what you need to do, it's up to you, and them now. My aim in writing this book was to help you by sharing my own and others' knowledge and experiences with you. To ease the burden on parents, help children transition better into school life and give teachers more time to just teach. I hope this book has helped you in some way, we are all different types of parents with different types of children but the advice I have shared with you should give you the confidence to successfully prepare your child for school. Good luck!

About the Author

Julie Dore is a primary school teacher, an author and a mother of two. Her husband is a Fly-In-Fly-Out (FIFO) worker and has been since 2006. Her daughters are five years old and nine months old. She has lived in Cairns, North Queensland, Australia most of her life, apart from a year she spent working and traveling in Canada and North America. Julie went to a local primary and high school and then went straight into studying Education at James Cook University. She has always loved working with children, so becoming a teacher was always on the cards for her. Julie found helping children to succeed, making learning fun and inspiring young minds each day very rewarding.

PREPPING FOR SCHOOL SUCCESS

She has a Bachelor of Education in Early Childhood Education and has been teaching in the Cairns area since 2005. Julie has taught Prep to Year 7 as well as pre-prep children locally and at a Montessori school in Canada. Her passion for reading children's books to her students led her to writing her own children's books. Then when her first daughter started Kindy she realised there was a lot she didn't know about school as a parent. It was like being on the other side of the fence and realising she was an amateur at this whole school parent thing. She had read quite a few parenting books as her daughters were growing up, but none had prepared her to be a successful school parent.

After teaching for 14 years she was the expert and knew schools inside and out but from a teacher's point of view, not a parent's. She had to learn the hard way by asking a lot of questions, re-asking questions, talking to other parents and searching on the Internet. That is where the idea to write her own book for parents came about. She saw there was a need to better prepare parents and their children for school. It is one of the longest things a child will do, as they can be in school from Kindy to Year 12 and that's 14 years of schooling! As a parent, she wished she had a book like *'Prepping for School Success'* to guide her through the early days. And as a teacher she wished parents and children already started school knowing the things in this book. It would have saved everyone a lot of time, effort and emotions. So, with some spare time, whilst she was on maternity leave from

ABOUT THE AUTHOR

teaching, she decided to write this book. A useful guide to help parents, children and teachers to not only survive school but thrive. Julie now spends her time working with parents and educators in her Prepping for Success presentations and workshops.

Author contact details

Julie Dore

Author | Educator | Speaker

Email: jdore1@hotmail.com
Author website: www.juliedore.com.au
Book website: www.preppingforschoolsuccess.com
Facebook: julie.dore.79230
Instagram: juliedore.author

Acknowledgements

Thanks to...

My mum Joan, for always being there for me and proofreading my book.

My daughter Claire, my illustrator, for her wonderful drawings on the front cover and throughout the book.

SPECIAL OFFERS

'Prepping for School Success- A Snapshot' Free PDF

Go to www.preppingforschoolsuccess.com to download your free PDF *'Prepping for School Success- A Snapshot'*. It's the must dos in dot points. Perfect for your other half who doesn't want to or have time to read this book. Or as my husband calls it, *'The pamphlet version'* or *'Dot points for Dads'*.

'Prepping for School Success' Private Facebook Group

Join my *'Prepping for School Success'* private Facebook Group for more tips, tricks and updates. Interact with other like-minded parents and educators in a safe, non-judgmental environment. Read other posts of interest or post your own questions or topics to discuss. Go to Facebook to join this exclusive group.

Julie Dore – Speaker

Julie Dore is an Author, Educator, Speaker and Mum. She has a Bachelor of Education (Early Childhood Education), 14 years teaching experience and two young children. Her experience, expertise and qualifications give her a comprehensive understanding of young children, parents and the education system. Julie is passionate about helping parents, children and educators be the best they can be. She has extensive experience speaking to groups of parents and other educators on a range of topics.

Julie is available to speak on the following topics:

- Positive Relationships
- Literacy & Numeracy Skills
- Routines & Organisation
- Life Skills Children Need
- Behaviour Management

Enquire about any of her 'Prepping for Success' Workshops:

✓ Successful Children:
- Essential Literacy & Numeracy Skills
- Important Life Hacks
- Developing the Whole Child

✓ Successful Parents:
- Awesome Routines & Organisation Tricks
- Positive Relationships
- Raising Amazing Children

✓ Successful Educators:
- Teaching the Whole Child
- Positive Relationships
- Effective Behaviour Management

Contact Julie at jdore1@hotmail.com to discuss how she can help you or your organisation today!

www.ingramcontent.com/pod-product-compliance
Lightning Source LLC
Chambersburg PA
CBHW031104080526
44587CB00011B/817